Little Kitchen

around the world

To my husband Anthony — thank you and enjoy.

Delicious international recipes that kids can really make

Little Kitchen
around
the world

Sabrina Parrini

Photography by John Laurie

SBS

hardie grant books
MELBOURNE · LONDON

Contents

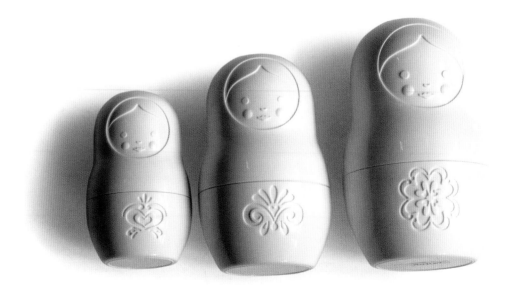

Sides

Biscuits & Cakes

Desserts

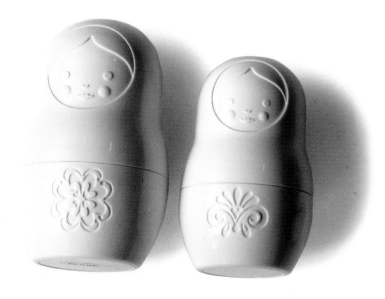

Dear Budding Chefs,

I absolutely LOVED writing this second book for you! Do you want to know why?

Well, one of the reasons is because, quite greedily, I'm the kind of person who will go to the effort of cooking myself a 'proper' meal even if I'm eating on my own.

I love nothing better than having good food to eat, day in day out. In writing this book, it's my hope that you also begin to realise that food you cook at home is well worth the effort. Not only is home-cooked food going to be better for you, I guarantee the recipes I've chosen for you here will taste better than fast food you grab on the run.

This book was also fun to write because it allowed me to travel around the world. Well, not literally you see, but figuratively … on a plate!

It was much cheaper than buying an around-the-world airline ticket but just as satisfying. I'm so happy you've joined me on this trip, because no matter what country you come from, I think you're really going to enjoy what's ahead. In my opinion, tasty food crosses all cultural boundaries.

While my first book was all about learning the basics and cooking good old favourites like shepherd's pie and pasta bake, this new cookbook is full of recipes from around the world.

Part of being a great cook is learning to experiment with new flavours and different ways of doing things in the kitchen. I hope that *Little Kitchen Around the World* teaches you some exciting new things and allows you to appreciate new tastes and flavours at the same time.

Hopefully, in years to come, as you become young adults you will always have these amazing recipes up your sleeve to cook not only for yourself, but for family and friends who drop in.

Happy cooking – have fun!

Sabrina

Dear Parents,

In this book you'll find recipes that I cooked with 7- to 12-year-old students at my children's cookery school. They have a decidedly multicultural feel, as that's what my students of this age group most seemed to appreciate. Cooking international food at home is in vogue, and the same goes for eating out. Nowadays, you'd be hard-pressed not to find a town with at least a few 'foreign' dining options available.

So what does this mean for the next generation? Well, for starters, it means they broaden their world-view, which is undoubtedly a good thing. Similarly, by eating a variety of foreign foods, we can more readily ensure our children are getting a bit of this and a bit of that – a balanced diet, as experts would recommend.

Generally, and I say this with some caution, I feel most cuisines are healthful. That is to say, they use vegetables and fruits abundantly and don't use excessive amounts of butter or cream.

In an age where everyone is talking childhood obesity, it is, of course, important to be sensible at the dining table. It is easy to get carried away and overindulge in foods we know, deep down, aren't good for us. However, my school of thought has always been to be 'real' when cooking and eating. I can't and won't turn a cold shoulder to butter, cream or salt in preparing my food. Like the next person, I try to be reasonable and of course don't eat these kinds of foods at every meal. There is, however, something to be said for not being too precious at the dinner table.

Eating should be pleasurable, as should cooking. Being too focused on limiting yourself takes the enjoyment out of cooking and ultimately eating. To me, eating well means eating food that at the end of the day tastes amazingly good. A large part of this 'taste' equation is eating foods from many different countries. Spices, marinades, rubs and grills from around the globe can pack such a flavour punch that they should not, in my book, be ignored, no matter how young or inexperienced your child!

So, please enthusiastically pass this book onto your budding chef and watch them broaden their culinary horizons. I hope you and your child relish cooking from this book. Think of it as your family's (very discounted) around-the-world airline ticket and me your multilingual hostess with the mostest.

Bon appetit!

Sabrina

Safety first

Attention adults!

While this cookbook aims to accurately describe what steps a child should be able to perform quite independently when cooking, you, as the supervising adult, should be close to hand at all times.

Please ask your child to wear mitts every time they use the oven and always use good judgement in the kitchen. A young, inexperienced child should never use a sharp knife, grater, peeler or food processor on their own. Of course, it is fine to allow children who are already familiar with kitchen equipment and cooking techniques to be more independent in the kitchen.

Please do spend some time showing your child how to use utensils and appliances several times over as they begin to learn to cook. Although fostering independence in the kitchen is a must, demonstrating and modelling how to properly use equipment at the outset is crucial.

When your child cooks their first few recipes, it's a great idea to be alongside them and demonstrate exactly how things are done and answer any questions that come up. And while autonomy in the kitchen is a good thing, I've found most children from 7 to 12 years still need kitchen guidance. Unexpected things can always happen to even the most seasoned cook!

Lastly, be relaxed and make kitchen time fun. Safety is important, but if you take too serious an approach all the pleasure will be lost and you'll end up with nervous budding chefs who are more likely to make mistakes!

A note about ovens

I use a fan-forced, convection oven to cook all of my recipes. Undoubtedly your oven will be different, so the recipes in this book might need slightly different cooking times to suit your situation. It's really important to get to know your oven well – ask your supervising adult to pass on any tips and tricks they know about how your particular oven works.

I always have an oven thermometer in my oven when cooking – I recommend you do the same. Oven thermometers can be bought cheaply at kitchenware stores and are a good investment. I always check my oven temperature before placing my dish in, to make sure the temperature is perfect before starting.

Also, I always have a shelf positioned in the middle of the oven before turning on the heat. All of my recipes should be cooked on the middle shelf (unless otherwise specified) to avoid any premature cooking or browning of food on the top shelf or any slow cooking on the bottom shelf.

Please also note …

Please exercise good judgement when using this book. Little Kitchen and the publisher take no responsibility for any injury caused while cooking or any allergic reactions that may eventuate as a result of using ingredients listed in this cookbook. It is the supervising adult's sole responsibility to ensure a child who has allergies doesn't cook a recipe that is inappropriate.

Ingredients

If you're like me, you're not only interested in cooking but also in hearing other people share their knowledge about it. For me, fun is watching chefs and cooks teach me something impressive on TV. I also love looking through cookbooks and food magazines because there is always something new to learn, no matter how long you've been cooking.

If the same goes for you, then I'm sure you have probably heard (or read) chefs on TV or in cookbooks and magazines talk about using the best quality ingredients that you can afford. That's because using a good-quality ingredient does affect the taste and sometimes even the look of your final product. Food is often richer, more flavourful and presents better if you are using a top-quality ingredient.

Here are some recommendations about the ingredients for the recipes in this book:

• Milk is full-cream.

• Eggs are 60 g, free-range and should be brought to room temperature before cooking.

• Onions are brown onions (unless otherwise specified).

• Cream is full-fat (low-fat cream does not whip).

• Meat is free-range and lean.

• Pepper is black pepper, finely ground.

• When cooking desserts, I use vanilla extract. You can also use vanilla-bean paste. I don't recommend using vanilla essence as it is imitation or fake vanilla (it is made from alcohol rather than pure vanilla).

• Butter (for baking) is unsalted.

Glossary of ingredients

Some of the ingredients in this book might be unfamiliar, but don't worry! There is a glossary of ingredients on page 114, which explains some of the more unusual or difficult-to-find ingredients. Ingredients that appear in the glossary have an asterisk next to them in the ingredients list on the recipe page.

Equipment

For each recipe you'll find a list of the equipment that you will need for preparing the ingredients.

Knives and chopping boards

Use a bigger knife for bigger ingredients and a smaller knife for small ingredients. Serrated knives are best for slicing bread. Remember that all knives should be kept sharp as blunt knives are more dangerous. Always use a chopping board when you are using a knife so that you don't scratch the bench or tabletop. It is important that the board doesn't slip around on the bench, so either use one that has a non-slip rubber base or rubber feet, or place a damp tea towel beneath the board to keep it steady. A bigger board is better, as you have more room to work on. Use two chopping boards if you need to prepare meat and vegetables in the same recipe.

Graters and peelers

Little chefs will find a box grater is easiest for grating and zesting. Conical graters and microplane zesters may be suitable for older children, but they do require a little more dexterity, because of their shape and the angle at which you need to hold the food. Try to use a grater that has a rubber handle on it and a non-slip rubber base to prevent accidents occurring due to loss of steadiness. It takes a bit of practice to use a peeler. Try to hold food steady on a chopping board and peel in long smooth movements, rather than little bits at a time.

Measuring jugs, measuring cups and measuring spoons

Although sometimes you will have to weigh an ingredient out using kitchen scales, wherever possible, I've suggested using measuring jugs, cups and spoons to measure ingredients. Don't use regular cups and spoons because they come in all sorts of different shapes and sizes, which means they won't be accurate.

This book uses standard Australian metric measures (1 tablespoon = 20 ml, 1 cup = 250 ml). American and European measures are a little bit different (1 tablespoon = 15 ml, 1 cup = 240 ml or 285 ml), so check your measuring equipment carefully to see which it is.

Jugs are for measuring liquids, like milk and stock. To measure accurately, sit the jug on the work surface and measure the ingredient to the marked line – not over or under it.

Cups are for measuring solid ingredients, like rice or flour. To measure accurately, heap the ingredient up high, then use a spatula to smooth over the top and make it level.

Spoons are for measuring smaller amounts of liquids or solids, such as honey or milk, baking powder or sugar. To measure accurately, heap the ingredient up high, then use a spatula to smooth over the top to make it level.

Mixing bowls

I recommend you have several different-sized mixing bowls – small, medium and large – to match the quantity of ingredients. Metal or plastic bowls are ideal as they are light and won't break if you drop them. Shallow bowls make mixing easier for children. When mixing in a bowl, use one hand to hold it steady on the bench and one hand to mix.

Food processor and electric mixer

Both these machines make kitchen work easier! Food processors are great for chopping ingredients quickly or turning them into a paste. Sometimes you have to scrape the ingredients down from the sides of the bowl so they mix in properly. Always make sure a grown-up puts in and removes the sharp blade and that they help you turn the machine on and off.

Electric mixers make cakes and biscuits easy. A grown-up should help you fit the correct attachment to the machine, help you set the correct speed and watch while you use it. A k-beater is used for beating, while a whisk is used to whip cream or egg whites.

Saucepans

I use a set of different-sized saucepans with a spout for easy pouring. Smaller saucepans are perfect for melting butter or chocolate, or for cooking smaller quantities. Use a large saucepan for cooking soup, pasta or rice. Saucepans should have a tight-fitting lid and a handle that won't get hot when you are cooking.

Frying pans

As the name suggests, these are for frying ingredients – often in a little bit of oil or butter. Non-stick pans are great because you can fry without oil and they are very easy to clean. Use a deeper pan for deep-frying. Some ingredients, such as nuts and spices, are dry-roasted without oil. Make sure your frying pans have a handle that won't get hot when you are cooking.

Colanders

These are used to drain boiled vegetables and pasta. Always ask a grown-up to help you and be careful to stand away from the hot steam. The safest way to drain hot items is to place the colander in the sink and pour the hot contents in.

Sieves and sifters

These have a fine mesh and are used to sift flour, icing sugar or cocoa to remove any lumps. They are often used when making cakes or batters, to ensure the mixture is smooth and light.

Oven

At Little Kitchen we use a fan-forced electric oven, and this is what we used to test the recipes in this book. Generally, fan-forced ovens cook faster than other ovens so you might need to adjust cooking temperatures and times if you have a conventional oven. Make sure you read the Safety First section on page 10 for more information about using ovens.

Baking trays, cake tins and muffin tins

Baking trays are metal trays for cooking things in the oven. Some are deep and are used for roasting meat. Shallow baking trays are used for cooking things like biscuits. Often, baking trays will need to be greased before use to stop food sticking. Use a piece of scrunched-up baking paper to rub the tray all over with a little butter or oil.

Cake tins and muffin tins come in different shapes and sizes. Make sure you use the correct size for the recipe you are preparing and grease or line it with baking paper, according to the instructions.

Baking dishes and ovenproof dishes

These are dishes that are able to be used in the oven without breaking. They are used for bakes, slices, casseroles and pies.

Wire racks

These are essential for cooling cakes or biscuits after they come out of the oven.

Pot holder

I use a large, non-slip pot holder (or trivet) to place hot dishes on. Always make sure pot holders are positioned on the table before your dish is to be served!

Kitchen timer

When cooking, I highly recommend using a kitchen timer to ensure that you cook the food for the correct amount of time. Some ovens have timers on them, but if yours doesn't, it's a good idea to go and buy one. They're available cheaply from most kitchenware stores.

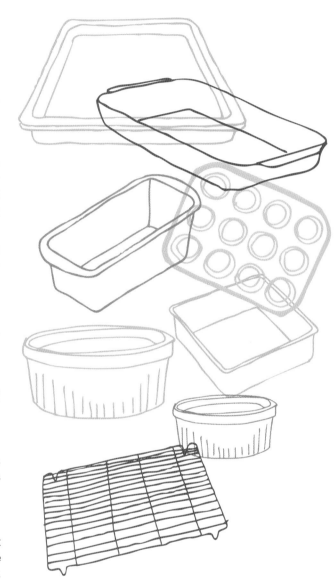

Utensils

Spoons can be wooden or metal and are used for stirring. In general, I recommend using spoons with long handles when stirring something in a pan on the stovetop to keep hands well away from hot contents.

Slotted spoons are useful for lifting solid ingredients, such as gnocchi, out of a liquid.

Tongs are perfect for moving things around in a frying pan or on the barbecue.

Whisks are used when you want to remove lumps to make a smooth sauce, or when you want to incorporate some air into ingredients such as cream or egg whites.

Spatulas and **palette knives** are perfect for scraping out bowls or for spreading fillings or icings onto cakes.

Egg flips are not just for eggs. They are useful for turning all sorts of things over in pans or for lifting them out.

Ladles are perfect for serving soups and stews as they hold more than spoons.

Biscuit cutters come in all sorts of shapes and sizes and are great for making biscuits or scones.

Pastry brushes are used to brush pastry with melted butter, egg or milk before baking, so that it turns golden and shiny. A brush can also be used to baste meat before and during cooking.

Plastic wrap comes in rolls and is used to wrap and seal food to stop it from drying out in the air.

Paper towel is absorbent paper that is used for mopping up spills in the kitchen or for draining food that has been fried.

Baking paper is often lightly coated in silicone and is used to line baking trays and cake tins so that biscuits or cakes won't stick.

Handy hints for budding chefs

When to cook?

Some of the dishes in this book are quick and easy to prepare, while others need more time and are a little trickier. To help you out, I've marked each recipe with an easy, medium or tricky icon. This way, you will know what you can easily cook after school, and what recipes are best left to weekends when you have more time to work through all of the steps carefully.

Ingredient preparation

Unlike my first book, which was for slightly younger children, the recipes in this cookbook require some ingredient preparation to be done beforehand. Each recipe's ingredients list will specify how an ingredient needs to be prepared before your cooking commences. For example, instead of saying '1 onion' in the ingredient list, the book will specify '1 onion, diced'.

Please ask an adult to help out when you're preparing food from the ingredients list and feel unsure about anything.

Staying safe

The recipes in this book often use sharp knives, an oven and/or a stovetop, which can be very dangerous. Please ask an adult to help you with these steps if you haven't had much experience with them or are unsure of how to use the equipment properly.

Useful cooking downloads

On pages 112 and 113 there are some useful Cooking Downloads that will help you to learn more about different techniques in the kitchen. I also encourage you and your parents to visit our cooking website:

www.littlekitchen.com.au

There you can download more useful tips and tricks in the form of our 'how to' cooking notes. If you're not already familiar with some preparation methods mentioned in this book, these notes will properly explain how to prepare the ingredients you're asked to cook with.

Lunch

French onion soup with cheesy croutons

France

Easy

4
Serves

The trick to getting the perfect colour to this soup is to caramelise the onions for as long as possible without burning them! Thinly slicing the onions takes a while and can sting your eyes, so ask an adult or friend to help with this step if you want to. The addition of the cheesy crouton on top of the soup, at the end, makes this even more delicious. If you don't like a thick, hearty soup, add an extra cup of beef stock when it's cooking.

Melt the butter in a large saucepan over medium heat. Add the onion and thyme leaves. Cover with a lid and cook, stirring regularly with a wooden spoon, for 45 minutes, or until the onion is soft and a rich golden brown. (If you don't stir the onions regularly they will stick to the bottom of the pan and go black!)

Add the flour and stir well. Cook for a further 2 minutes. Add the stock, sugar and mustard. Partially cover the pan with the lid and bring to the boil.

While it is coming to the boil, preheat the oven to 180°C (Gas 4).

Reduce the heat to low and simmer for 30 minutes, scraping the base of the saucepan to remove any caramelised bits (to find out what simmering is, see page 112).

While the soup is cooking, make the croutons. Arrange the baguette slices on a baking tray and place on the middle shelf of the oven for 8 minutes, or until lightly golden.

Wearing oven mitts, remove the tray from the oven. Top each baguette slice with an even amount of cheese. Put the slices back into the oven and heat for a further 10 minutes, or until the cheese is golden.

When the soup is ready, ladle it into bowls and serve with two croutons per person.

50 g **butter**

1 kg **brown onions,** halved and thinly sliced

2 **thyme sprigs,** leaves only

2 tablespoons **plain flour**

2 **beef stock cubes,** dissolved in 1 litre boiling water

1 tablespoon **brown sugar**

2 tablespoons **dijon mustard**

8 slices of **baguette,** about 2 cm thick

¾ cup grated **cheddar cheese**

EQUIPMENT

large saucepan with lid

sharp knife

chopping board

wooden spoon

measuring spoons

measuring jug

measuring cups

baking tray

oven mitts

grater

ladle

Mange de la soupe

20

Oishii udon

Udon noodle salad

400 g dried **udon noodles***, snapped in half

80 g **sugar snap peas**

4 **spring onions**, thinly sliced

⅓ cup chopped **mint leaves**

1 tablespoon **sesame seeds**

⅓ cup **fried shallots***

DRESSING

2 tablespoons **sesame oil**

2 **garlic cloves**, crushed

2 tablespoons **soy sauce**

1 tablespoon **rice wine vinegar**

1 tablespoon **mirin***

1 tablespoon finely grated **ginger**

1½ teaspoons **lime juice**

¼ cup **brown sugar**

EQUIPMENT

medium saucepan

colander

sharp knife

chopping board

large mixing bowl

measuring spoons

measuring cups

frying pan

wooden spoon

grater

tongs

Japan

Medium

4 Serves

This is, without a doubt, one of my favourite recipes. Not only are the ingredients super healthy, the dish also packs an incredible flavour punch. Most people recommend eating udon noodle salad cold, but I prefer it warm, as the aromas of the ingredients come out while you're eating it! You can also add shredded chicken or thinly sliced lamb if you want to make it more substantial. Fried shallots are available from the Asian section of supermarkets.

Place the noodles in a medium saucepan and pour in boiling water until it reaches three-quarters of the way up the pan. Cook the noodles over medium heat for about 6 minutes or until they are just tender. Place a colander in the sink, then drain the noodles.

Remove the stems from the sugar snap peas and slice lengthways into thin julienne strips (see page 112 to find out how to julienne).

Place the sugar snap peas, spring onion and mint in a large bowl. Put the noodles on top but don't mix (the heat from the noodles will partially cook the vegetables and herbs).

To make the dressing, put the sesame oil into a frying pan and place over medium heat. Add the garlic and fry, stirring well with a wooden spoon, for 2 minutes, or until just golden.

Remove the pan from the heat. Add the soy sauce, vinegar, mirin, ginger, lime juice and sugar. Stir until the sugar has dissolved, then pour the dressing over the noodles. Toss well with tongs to combine.

Divide the noodles into four bowls. Sprinkle 1 teaspoon of the sesame seeds and 1 tablespoon of the fried shallots over each bowl and serve immediately.

Japan is made up of four islands that are located in an area that's known as the Ring of Fire. Because of this volatile location, Japan experiences over 1,000 earthquakes every year.

Tuna couscous

Morocco

Easy

4 Serves

Light and refreshing but deeply satisfying, this couscous dish makes a delicious and quick meal if you don't feel like something too heavy. Take it on a picnic or to school as part of a flavour-packed lunch! You could also add chopped tomatoes, gherkins or olives to this dish.

Put the couscous in a large heatproof bowl. Pour the boiling water over the couscous and lightly stir with a fork. Securely cover the bowl with plastic wrap and stand for 5 minutes, or until all the water has been absorbed.

Gently fluff up the couscous with a fork to separate. Add the onion, capers, tuna, chives and parsley. Pour over the olive oil and lemon juice, then season with the salt and pepper. Stir the couscous thoroughly with a fork, then serve either warm or cold.

1 cup instant **couscous***

1 cup **boiling water**

1 small **red onion**, halved and thinly sliced

¼ cup salted **capers**, rinsed thoroughly

1 x 185 g can of **tuna** in oil, drained and finely flaked

2 tablespoons finely snipped **chives**

2 tablespoons finely chopped **parsley leaves**

¼ cup **extra-virgin olive oil**

2 tablespoons **lemon juice**

½ teaspoon **salt**

2 pinches of **black pepper**

EQUIPMENT

measuring cups

large heatproof bowl

fork

plastic wrap

sharp knife

chopping board

measuring spoons

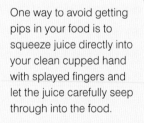
One way to avoid getting pips in your food is to squeeze juice directly into your clean cupped hand with splayed fingers and let the juice carefully seep through into the food.

Mushroom quiche

1 teaspoon **butter**, for greasing

2 sheets of **puff pastry**

1 **onion**, peeled and halved

1 tablespoon **olive oil**

450 g **button mushrooms**, thinly sliced

¼ cup **thickened cream**

4 eggs

1 cup grated **cheddar cheese**

2 **spring onions**, thinly sliced

2 tablespoons finely snipped **chives**

2 pinches of **salt**

2 pinches of **black pepper**

EQUIPMENT

25 cm springform quiche tin

baking paper

sharp knife

ruler

pie weights, dried beans or rice

oven mitts

fork

food processor

chopping board

measuring spoons

large frying pan with lid

mixing bowls

wooden spoon

measuring cups

grater

whisk

ladle

palette knife

France

Medium

Serves

I love making quiches not only because they're simple to cook, but also because they really are incredibly tasty for the little effort you put in. You can use lots of different fillings in quiches – ham and cheese, grilled vegetables, bacon and leek, and, of course, mushroom!

Preheat the oven to 180°C (Gas 4). Grease a 25 cm springform quiche tin with the butter, using some scrunched-up baking paper.

Position 1 pastry sheet underneath the quiche tin. Using a sharp knife, cleanly cut all around the tin, making a circle. Place this pastry circle in the base of the tin, making sure no air bubbles are caught underneath!

Next, using a sharp knife and a ruler, measure out and cut three identical pastry strips that are 26 cm long and 5 cm wide. Position these strips so they stick together right around the inside wall of the tin and join the bottom pastry circle. Use your fingers to press down any places where the different pieces of pastry join and overlap.

Line the pastry with a large sheet of baking paper and completely fill the tin with pie weights, dried beans or rice. Place the tin on the middle shelf of the oven. Bake the pastry for 10 minutes, or until lightly golden (this is called blind baking, see page 112 to read more about it).

Carefully remove the tin from the oven using oven mitts and cool for 5 minutes. Tip the pie weights, dried beans or rice into a bowl. Remove and discard the paper.

Use the tines (teeth) of a fork to prick the pastry base and sides about 40 times. Carefully return the pastry shell to the oven using oven mitts and bake for another 8 minutes, or until the pastry is lightly golden. When ready, remove the tin from the oven using oven mitts and set aside to cool.

Place the onion in a food processor and blitz to a fine paste (for extra information on how to do this, see page 113).

Put the olive oil in a frying pan and place over medium heat. Add the onion paste and mushrooms and stir with a wooden spoon to combine. Place a lid on the frying pan and cook for a couple of minutes. Remove the lid and continue cooking for 10 minutes, or until all the liquid has evaporated. Set aside to cool.

In the meantime, put the cream in a bowl. Add the eggs and whisk well. Add the cheese, spring onion, chives, salt, pepper and mushrooms and mix well. Using a ladle, pour the mixture into the pastry case.

Bake for 40–45 minutes, or until a knife inserted into the quiche comes out clean and the top is golden.

Remove the quiche from the tin and place on a platter. Allow it to rest for 10 minutes before slicing into wedges and serving warm (for tips on how to slice, see page 112).

Frijole nachos

Mexico

Easy

4 Serves

'Frijole' is the Mexican word for 'bean'. This recipe is meat-free but is still really tasty and hearty because of the bean base. I usually serve nachos with the toppings on the side rather than sloppily piled on top. This way, the nachos don't go all soggy underneath! This is a quick and easy recipe you can make with your friends.

Preheat the oven to 180°C (Gas 4).

Evenly divide the refried beans between four ovenproof plates. Next, arrange the corn chips by standing them up vertically on the beans. Evenly sprinkle on the cheese.

Put the plates on a baking tray and place it on the middle shelf of the oven. Cook the nachos for 15 minutes, or until the cheese is melted but not crisp.

In the meantime, spoon the salsa, sour cream and guacamole into three bowls. Place the bowls in the middle of the table with serving spoons and place a pot holder at each person's spot.

When the nachos are ready, use oven mitts to carefully remove the plates from the oven and place on the table. Eat the nachos straight away, spooning on as much salsa, sour cream and guacamole as you like. Just be careful not to burn yourself on the plates!

1 x 435 g can of **refried beans**

1 x 230 g bag of **corn chips**

1 cup grated **cheddar cheese**

1 small jar of **tomato salsa** (mild, medium or spicy depending on your taste)

1 x 200 g tub of **sour cream**

1 quantity of fresh **guacamole** (see page 70)

EQUIPMENT

ovenproof plates

grater

large baking tray

oven mitts

Did you know that people in Mexico and the USA celebrate International Day of the Nacho every year on the 21st of October?

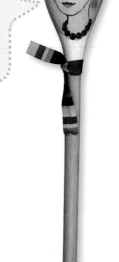

Blackened Cajun chicken sandwich

CAJUN SPICE
1 teaspoon **hot paprika**
1 teaspoon **garlic powder**
1 teaspoon **dried oregano**
1 teaspoon **salt**

1 teaspoon **butter**, for greasing
250 g **chicken breast fillet**, skin and fat removed
1 tablespoon **olive oil**
1 tablespoon **butter**
2 **panini buns**
2 tablespoons **mayonnaise**
2 slices of **cheddar cheese**
1 **iceberg lettuce leaf**, halved
1 small **red onion**, thinly sliced into rings
1 **tomato**, thinly sliced

EQUIPMENT
measuring spoons
small mixing bowl
baking trays
sharp knives
meat tenderiser
chopping board
large plate
pastry brush
frying pan
tongs
baking paper
butter knife
oven mitts

To save time, you could buy the Cajun spice mix from the supermarket.

USA

Easy

2

Serves

The first time I had one of these sandwiches was at an American diner – it was served with a side of fries and ketchup (tomato sauce). This is a super-tasty sandwich but it's not for the faint-hearted! The Cajun mix is pretty spicy, so only sprinkle a little of it on your meat if you don't like spicy food!

To make the Cajun spice, simply mix all the ingredients in a bowl.

Preheat the oven to 180ºC (Gas 4) and grease a baking tray with the butter, using some scrunched-up baking paper.

Using a sharp knife, slice the chicken breast in half lengthways. Next, slice both pieces of chicken in half widthways so that you have four pieces of chicken.

Tenderise the chicken pieces by bashing them on both sides with a meat tenderiser until they are quite flat. Set the chicken aside, then thoroughly wash and dry your hands.

Scatter the Cajun spice on a large plate and put the olive oil in a small dish. Generously brush both sides of the chicken with the oil and coat each piece in the spice mix by pressing down firmly.

Melt the butter in a frying pan over high heat. Cook the chicken pieces for 1 minute on each side. Be careful not to overcook the chicken, as it will become tough. The butter may blacken from the Cajun spice mix, but don't worry as that's normal!

Next, remove the chicken using tongs, and place onto the greased baking tray. Cook on the middle shelf of the oven for around 5 minutes, or until just cooked through.

In the meantime, slice each panini bun in half lengthways. Spread 1 tablespoon of the mayonnaise on the inside (top and bottom) of each bun and place a slice of cheese on the top half. On the bottom half, arrange a piece of lettuce leaf, some onion rings and 2–3 slices of tomato.

When the chicken is ready, use oven mitts to remove the tray from the oven. Arrange 2 pieces of chicken on each bun base using tongs. Put the lid on each burger and place them back on the baking tray. Using oven mitts, return them to the oven for another 3 minutes to melt the cheese.

Remove the tray from the oven using oven mitts and serve the sandwiches immediately alongside some crispy fries and tomato sauce.

Red onion and orange salad

Spain

Easy

Serves

This salad is a firm favourite in Spain. Served chilled, it is tangy and sweet at the same time. When I make this, I pop all the ingredients in the fridge for several hours ahead of time. That way, there's no need to chill the salad after the preparation is done! You could also substitute one of the regular oranges with a red blood orange for a really spectacular result!

Peel the oranges and remove the white pith. Slice each orange widthways into ½ cm thick slices and remove as many pips as possible.

Arrange the slices on a serving platter, overlapping them slightly, and evenly scatter over the red onion.

In a small bowl, whisk together the orange juice, vinegar, olive oil and salt.

Spoon the dressing over the onion and oranges and serve.

5 small **oranges**
(seville or navel are best)

½ small **red onion,**
very thinly sliced

1 tablespoon freshly squeezed
orange juice

½ teaspoon **raspberry***
or **red wine vinegar**

1 tablespoon **extra-virgin
olive oil**

1 pinch of **salt**

EQUIPMENT

sharp knife

chopping board

serving platter

measuring spoons

small mixing bowl

whisk

metal tablespoon

If you're feeling adventurous, you could garnish this salad with ⅓ cup of pitted kalamata olives and ⅓ cup of roughly crumbled Greek feta cheese. This might sound like an unusual combination, but it is really delicious!

Dinner

Chicken cacciatore

½ cup **plain flour**

1 kg **chicken thighs**, skin and fat removed

¼ cup **olive oil**

1 large **onion**, peeled and halved

3 **garlic cloves**, crushed

1 **red capsicum** (pepper)

300 g **button mushrooms**, sliced

1 x 400 g can of diced **tomatoes**

1 **bay leaf**

300 ml **chicken stock**

1 cup pitted **kalamata olives**

EQUIPMENT

measuring cups

large plate

measuring spoons

large casserole dish with lid

tongs

wooden spoon

food processor

measuring jug

sharp knife

chopping board

Italy

Medium

6

Serves

Chicken cacciatore is nutritious and bursts with flavour. If you like, you can make this recipe ahead of time, cool it and keep it in the fridge for a couple of days before serving. It also freezes successfully.

Put the flour on a large plate. Using your hands, coat the chicken pieces thoroughly on both sides.

Put 1 tablespoon of the olive oil in a large flameproof casserole dish and place over medium heat. Using tongs, add half the chicken pieces and cook for 10 minutes, or until browned all over. Repeat for the next batch, using a second tablespoon of the olive oil. Transfer the cooked chicken onto a plate and set aside.

Place the onion and garlic in a food processor and blitz to a fine paste (for extra information on how to do this, see page 113).

Halve the capsicum and remove the seeds. Slice lengthways into thin julienne strips (see page 112 to find out how to julienne).

Measure the remaining tablespoon of oil into the casserole dish and place over medium heat. Add the onion and garlic paste and fry, stirring occasionally with a wooden spoon, for 5 minutes, or until golden. Add the capsicum and mushrooms, cover with a lid and cook for a further 5 minutes.

Return the chicken pieces to the casserole dish. Add the tomatoes, bay leaf and stock and stir well. Reduce the heat to low and cook, covered, for 30 minutes, stirring occasionally. Add the olives and cook for a further 10 minutes, or until the sauce has thickened.

Serve the chicken cacciatore with some creamy mashed potato.

Did you know that the Italian word 'cacciatore' means hunter? So the name of this dish can be translated to 'hunter-style chicken'!

Moussaka

Greece

Tricky

6 Serves

I like to think of moussaka as the Greek cousin of Italian lasagne. They're similar in that they use flavoured minced meat that has been layered with other ingredients and then baked in the oven. This is perfect winter food, but be warned – it does take some time to prepare! I like to use small eggplants in this dish as they're sweeter and less woody than their big counterparts.

Place the eggplant on a chopping board. Using your fingers, rub the salt all over the slices, then place them in a colander. Position the colander in the sink and leave for 20 minutes. (This will draw out any bitterness from the eggplant.) Rinse the eggplant well under cold running water, then pat dry with a tea towel.

In the meantime, melt the butter in a large frying pan over medium heat until just golden. Add the mince and stir well with a wooden spoon. Cook for 8–10 minutes, or until browned all over, then set aside in a small bowl.

Put the olive oil in the frying pan and cook the onion and garlic over medium heat for 5 minutes, or until golden brown. Add the tomatoes, spices, salt, pepper, stock and mince and mix well. Cook, stirring occasionally, for about 20 minutes, or until the sauce thickens.

Preheat the oven to 200°C (Gas 6).

Beat the eggs in a small mixing bowl and spread the flour out on a large plate. Dip the slices of eggplant into the egg, then coat them in the flour. Repeat until all the eggplant slices have been coated. (Your hands will get sticky so wash them several times throughout the process.)

Heat 2 tablespoons of olive oil in a clean frying pan over low–medium heat and fry the eggplant until golden on both sides. Continue to fry the eggplant in batches, using 2 tablespoons of oil each time. (Watch for splattering when you first place the eggplant pieces in the oil.) Drain the fried eggplant on paper towel.

To make the white sauce, melt the butter in a medium saucepan over medium heat. Add the flour and whisk for 30 seconds (this paste is called a 'roux'). Gradually pour in the milk, whisking constantly. Keep on vigorously whisking for 6–7 minutes, or until you have a smooth, thick sauce. Remove from the heat and set aside.

Use half of the eggplant to cover the bottom of your baking dish. Next, spoon on half of the mince. Repeat this process with the remainder of the eggplant and mince. Spoon the white sauce on top, then sprinkle over the cheese.

Bake the moussaka on the middle shelf of the oven for 1 hour, or until the top is golden brown. Remove from the oven using oven mitts and leave to cool for 5 minutes before cutting it into squares and serving.

2 **eggplants** (aubergine) (about 600 g in total), sliced into 1 cm thick slices

⅓ cup **salt**

10 g **butter**

700 g **lamb mince**

1 tablespoon **olive oil**

1 large **onion**, finely chopped

2 **garlic cloves**, crushed

1 x 400 g can of diced **tomatoes**

½ teaspoon **ground cinnamon**

½ teaspoon **ground nutmeg**

1 teaspoon **salt**

½ teaspoon **black pepper**

1 cup **beef stock**

2 **eggs**

1 cup **plain flour**

extra **olive oil**, for frying

WHITE SAUCE

70 g **butter**

½ cup **plain flour**

3 cups **milk**

2 pinches of **ground nutmeg**

1 cup grated **cheddar cheese**

EQUIPMENT

sharp knife

chopping board

measuring cups

colander

tea towel

2 large frying pans

wooden spoon

mixing bowls

measuring spoons

large plate

whisk

tongs

paper towel

medium saucepan

grater

baking dish, 30 cm x 22 cm x 6 cm

2 large, metal spoons

oven mitts

egg flip or spatula

Preserved lemon roast chicken

4 **chicken thighs**, skin on
4 **chicken drumsticks**, skin on
500 ml **buttermilk**
8 pieces of **preserved lemon***
1 teaspoon **olive oil**
3 **thyme sprigs**, leaves only
½ teaspoon **black pepper**

EQUIPMENT
square baking dish, 25 cm x
25 cm x 6 cm high
measuring jug
tongs
plastic wrap
medium mixing bowl
strainer
measuring spoons
foil
oven mitts

Morocco

Easy

4
Serves

Making the perfect roast chicken is something that puzzles many people. I often find it much easier just to cook chicken pieces in the oven, as my mother did when I was younger, rather than a whole chook. I use a Moroccan staple – preserved lemons – when making roast chicken as I love the briny tartness they add to food. Use chicken thighs and drumsticks instead of breast fillets, as they'll remain wonderfully soft and tender throughout the cooking process. Also, start this recipe the night before if you can – marinating the chicken overnight will make a world of difference to the end result.

Place the chicken thighs and drumsticks in a 25 cm square baking dish and pour over the buttermilk. Mix well with tongs. Cover with plastic wrap and place in the fridge to marinate for at least 1 hour, or overnight. Turn the chicken over once during the marinating process.

Preheat the oven to 180°C (Gas 4).

Put the preserved lemon in a bowl, cover with warm water and soak for 10 minutes. Drain and set aside.

Take the chicken pieces out of the baking dish and wash them under cold water to remove the excess buttermilk. Rinse the baking dish, then return the chicken pieces to it.

Drizzle the olive oil over the chicken pieces. Scatter over the thyme leaves and pepper, then arrange the preserved lemon on top. Cover the baking dish with foil, place on the middle shelf of the oven and cook for 15 minutes.

Remove the dish using oven mitts and turn the chicken pieces over with tongs. Cover with foil once more and return to the oven for another 15 minutes.

Carefully remove the foil from the dish, then cook for a further 15 minutes, or until the chicken skin is crisp and golden and the chicken is cooked through.

Serve the roast chicken with a simple salad of tomatoes and herbs. It can also be enjoyed cold the next day!

Just over 32 million people live in Morocco, which is roughly half the size of New South Wales in Australia, or about the same size of California in the USA!

Eggplant and potato curry

India

Medium

Serves

I really love this dish. I think it is a bit like Indian comfort food — flavoursome and earthy, rich and satisfying. It is especially good for the colder months and delicious served alongside some steamed basmati rice and a rogan josh curry.

Put 2 tablespoons of the oil in a frying pan and place over medium heat. Add the mustard seeds, chilli powder, garam masala and Madras curry powder and stir well. Cook for 2 minutes, or until the seeds start to pop.

Add the eggplant and cook, stirring regularly with a wooden spoon, for about 15 minutes, or until golden. Use a slotted spoon to remove the eggplant from the frying pan and put in a bowl. Set aside.

Put the remaining oil in the same frying pan and place over medium heat. Add the onion and garlic and fry, stirring regularly, for 5 minutes, or until golden. Stir through the tomatoes, stock, salt and sugar. Reduce the heat to low–medium, then cover and simmer for 20 minutes.

Next, add the potatoes. Simmer, stirring occasionally, for another 15 minutes, or until the potatoes are just tender but not breaking apart. Add the eggplant and 1 cup of water. Cook for a further 15 minutes, or until the potatoes and eggplants are tender but not mushy and the sauce has thickened.

Serve the curry straight away with raita.

¼ cup **vegetable oil**

2 teaspoons **black mustard seeds**

½ teaspoon **chilli powder**

½ teaspoon **garam masala*** (see recipe on page 58)

½ teaspoon **Madras curry powder***

1 **eggplant** (aubergine), cut into 2 cm cubes

1 large **onion,** finely chopped

2 **garlic cloves,** crushed

1 x 400 g can of diced **tomatoes**

1 cup **vegetable stock**

1 teaspoon **salt**

1 teaspoon **sugar**

500 g all-purpose **potatoes,** peeled and cut into 2 cm cubes

EQUIPMENT

measuring spoons

large frying pan with lid

wooden spoon

slotted spoon

medium mixing bowl

measuring cups

Raita is an Indian condiment that is really easy to prepare. Dry-roast 1 teaspoon of ground cumin in a frying pan over medium heat for around 30 seconds. Once cooled, add the cumin to 200 g of yoghurt along with 1 small grated cucumber and 1 teaspoon of crushed garlic.

Prawn and tomato paella

2 tablespoons **olive oil**
1 large **onion,** finely chopped
2 **garlic cloves,** crushed
½ **red capsicum** (pepper), thinly sliced
1 cup **vialone nano rice***
3 cups **beef stock**
4 **saffron threads**
1 x 400 g can of diced **tomatoes**
1 teaspoon **red capsicum paste***
1 teaspoon **salt**
1 tablespoon finely chopped **parsley leaves**
4 **lemon wedges,** to serve

GARLIC PRAWNS
16 small, **green prawns,** shelled and deveined
50 g **butter**
1 tablespoon **olive oil**
1 **garlic clove,** crushed

EQUIPMENT
measuring spoons
sharp knife
chopping board
paella pan (a large frying pan is fine as well)
wooden spoon
measuring cups
measuring jug
8 skewers
large grill pan

Spain

Medium

Serves

This is my version of paella. Ask any Spanish person and they will probably say that it's not the authentic way of making it, but I find this method easy and the results are just as delicious. The red capsicum paste can be bought from some supermarkets and Middle Eastern stores. It's not essential but does give the paella an interesting flavour.

Put the olive oil in a paella pan (or large frying pan) and place over medium heat. Add the onion, garlic and capsicum. Cook, stirring occasionally with a wooden spoon, for 5 minutes, or until the garlic and onion are lightly golden.

Add the rice and cook, stirring constantly, for about 5 minutes, or until the rice is completely coated in oil and is a little translucent.

Add the stock, saffron, tomatoes, capsicum paste and salt. Cook, stirring regularly, over low heat for 25 minutes, or until the rice is 'al dente' (for tips on how to check if something is 'al dente', see page 113).

In the meantime, prepare the garlic prawns. Take eight wooden skewers and thread two prawns onto each one. Heat the butter and oil in a large grill pan over high heat. Add the garlic and cook, stirring constantly, for 30 seconds, or until fragrant but not yet golden.

Add the prawn skewers and cook them for about 2 minutes on each side, or until just cooked (the prawns will turn white when cooked).

Pile the skewers on top of the paella and scatter with the parsley. Serve straight away with the lemon wedges.

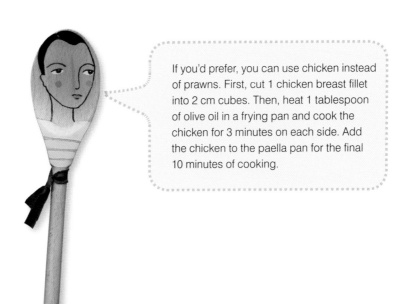

If you'd prefer, you can use chicken instead of prawns. First, cut 1 chicken breast fillet into 2 cm cubes. Then, heat 1 tablespoon of olive oil in a frying pan and cook the chicken for 3 minutes on each side. Add the chicken to the paella pan for the final 10 minutes of cooking.

47

Lamb souvlaki

Greece

Medium

4 Serves

Healthy, super tasty and easy to cook, I promise you this souvlaki will be better than any other you've eaten. Have it for lunch or dinner, but just remember to have a napkin nearby, as the lamb can get a bit juicy!

Preheat the oven to 180°C (Gas 4).

Place the lamb in a ceramic baking dish. Add 1 tablespoon of the olive oil, along with the lemon juice, oregano, garlic, finely chopped onion and pepper to the meat. Mix well using tongs. Cover the dish with plastic wrap, then refrigerate for at least 20 minutes, or up to 2 hours.

Put another tablespoon of the olive oil in a frying pan and place over medium heat. Add the thinly sliced onion and salt and cook, stirring regularly with a wooden spoon, for 10 minutes, or until the onion is golden and just tender. Set aside.

Remove the lamb from the fridge and discard the plastic wrap. Put the last tablespoon of the olive oil on a cast iron grill and place over medium heat. Drain the meat well using a slotted spoon, then grill it for 3 minutes on each side, or until just cooked through.

While the meat is cooking, put the souvlaki bread on a baking tray and place in the oven for 3 minutes, or until soft. Remove the bread from the oven using oven mitts and transfer to four serving plates.

Spoon 1 tablespoon of tzatziki onto the middle of each souvlaki bread and spread it vertically up and down with a metal tablespoon. Evenly divide the meat between the souvlaki breads, then top with the onion, lettuce and tomato.

Tightly roll the souvlaki so that they resemble sausages. Place them seam side down on the serving plates and eat immediately!

400 g **lamb**, trimmed and cut into 3 cm long strips

¼ cup **olive oil**

¼ cup **lemon juice**

1 tablespoon **dried oregano**

3 **garlic cloves**, crushed

1 small **onion**, finely chopped

2 pinches of **black pepper**

1 large **onion**, thinly sliced

½ teaspoon **salt**

4 **souvlaki breads***

⅓ cup **tzatziki***

1 large **iceberg lettuce leaf**, shredded

1 large **tomato**, thinly sliced

EQUIPMENT

sharp knife

chopping board

ceramic baking dish

measuring spoons

measuring cups

tongs

plastic wrap

frying pan

wooden spoon

cast iron grill

slotted spoon

baking tray

oven mitts

metal tablespoon

nostimos!

Pad Thai

3 **eggs**
2 tablespoons **vegetable oil**
2 **garlic cloves**, crushed
1 **red capsicum**
12 **fresh baby corns**, halved
1 teaspoon **soy sauce**
1 teaspoon **fish sauce**
2 teaspoons **sugar**
1 teaspoon **lime juice**
1 tablespoon **tamarind paste***
½ teaspoon **chilli powder**
200 g **thick rice noodles**
3 **spring onions**, white part only,
finely chopped
¼ cup **crushed peanuts**
4 **lime wedges**

EQUIPMENT

medium mixing bowls
whisk
measuring spoons
wok
large plate
sharp knife
chopping board
large metal spoon
medium saucepan
colander
measuring cups

Thailand

Medium

Serves

Pad Thai is one of the most popular Thai dishes. It's known as 'street food' and in Bangkok you'll find heaps of street-side food-carts making it right in front of you. Many slight variations feature on menus all over the world, but it always contains rice noodles accompanied by some form of vegetable, nuts and in some cases tofu, meat or seafood.

Whisk the eggs in a bowl until frothy. Add 1 tablespoon of the oil into a wok and place over medium heat. Add the egg, swirl it around the wok and cook for 3 minutes. Lightly scramble the egg by running your whisk through it and cook for a further 2 minutes, or until just set. Remove from the wok, put on a plate and set aside.

Halve the capsicum and remove the seeds and stem. Slice widthways into thin julienne strips (see page 112 to find out how to julienne).

Warm the remaining tablespoon of oil in the wok over medium heat. Add the garlic and cook, stirring well with a large metal spoon, for about 30 seconds, or until just golden.

Add the capsicum and baby corn and cook for about 10 minutes, or until the vegetables are just tender.

Add the soy sauce, fish sauce, sugar, lime juice, tamarind paste and chilli powder. Stir well, turn off the heat and set aside.

Fill a saucepan with boiling water and place over high heat until it reaches a rolling boil (see page 112 for more information on the different ways you can boil something). Add the noodles and cook for about 6 minutes, or until just tender. They shouldn't be so soft that they fall apart.

Drain the noodles in a colander, then add them to the wok along with the egg and spring onion. Reduce the heat to low–medium and gently warm the noodles for a few minutes, taking care when mixing everything so the noodles don't get broken.

Divide the noodles into bowls or takeaway boxes. Sprinkle over the peanuts, arrange the lime wedges on top and eat straight away.

Spinach and ricotta cannelloni

Italy

Tricky

6–8
Serves

This vegetarian dish is so delicous that it will win over even the biggest meat lover.

Make the sauce

Place the onion and garlic in a food processor and blitz to a fine paste (for extra information on how to do this, see page 113).

Put the olive oil in a medium saucepan and place over medium heat. Add the onion and garlic paste and fry for 5 minutes, or until lightly golden, stirring from time to time. Add the tomatoes, ½ can of water, sugar, salt and bicarbonate of soda and stir well. Partially cover with a lid and cook, stirring regularly, for 35 minutes, or until reduced to a thick sauce.

Put the lasagne sheets in a large bowl and pour over enough boiling water to cover them completely. Soak for 10 minutes, moving them around regularly with tongs to prevent them from sticking, then remove and lay out on two clean, damp tea towels.

Make the ricotta mix

Fill a large saucepan with boiling water and place over high heat until it reaches a rolling boil (see page 112 for more information on boiling and simmering).

Remove the stems from the spinach and wash the leaves thoroughly. Put the spinach in a steamer, then place over the saucepan of boiling water. Reduce the heat to medium and steam for 15 minutes, or until the spinach has wilted. Remove the steamer and run the spinach under cold water for 30 seconds, then set aside.

Wash your hands well, then crumble the ricotta into a large bowl. Add the spinach, salt, pepper and nutmeg and mix well using your hands.

Assemble and cook the cannelloni

Preheat the oven to 180°C (Gas 4). Take the two tea towels with the laid-out lasagne sheets. Put ½ cup of ricotta mix in the middle of each lasagne sheet. Using your hands, shape the ricotta mix so that it resembles a sausage, making sure that it runs the whole way down the longest length of the lasagne sheet. Repeat for each lasagne sheet.

Next, using both hands, fold each side of the lasagne sheet inwards over the ricotta, so that the edges of the sheet overlap and you're left with a tight log shape. Repeat until all the cannelloni are rolled, then transfer to a chopping board.

Using a sharp knife, carefully slice the cannelloni in half, so that you have 2 small cannelloni. (The pasta will be a bit hard to cut through so ask for help if you are having trouble.)

Cover the bases of three baking dishes, each 22 cm x 22 cm, with a little of the tomato sauce. Place 6 cannelloni in each dish and use the rest of the tomato sauce to cover them. Sprinkle the cheese evenly over the cannelloni. Bake on the middle and bottom shelves of the oven for 30 minutes, or until the cheese is melted and lightly golden.

Remove the baking dishes from the oven using oven mitts and place on the table. Serve immediately, with an egg flip beside each dish for people to help themselves.

1 **onion**, peeled and halved

2 **garlic cloves**, peeled

1 tablespoon **olive oil**

2 x 400 g cans of diced **tomatoes**

½ teaspoon **sugar**

1 teaspoon **salt**

tiny pinch of **bicarbonate of soda**

9 instant **lasagne sheets**

350 g **baby spinach**

950 g fresh **ricotta**

1 tablespoon **salt**

1 pinch of **black pepper**

2 pinches of **ground nutmeg**

2 cups grated **cheddar cheese**

EQUIPMENT

food processor

medium saucepan with lid

wooden spoon

measuring spoons

large mixing bowls

tongs

tea towels

large saucepan with lid and steamer

measuring cups

large chopping board

sharp knife

3 baking dishes, 22 cm x 22 cm

grater

oven mitts

egg flip

Cannelloni is great served with a fresh garden salad! They can also be frozen and reheated later.

Girello pot roast

2 tablespoons **olive oil**

1 large piece of **girello***
(silverside), fat removed

1 large **onion**, quartered

4 **garlic cloves**, peeled

1 **beef stock cube**

2 **bay leaves**

10 whole **cloves**

1 teaspoon **salt**

2 pinches of **black pepper**

EQUIPMENT

measuring spoons

large stockpot with lid

sharp knife

measuring jug

long-handled tongs

chopping board

large slotted spoon

When I was younger, my mother made this dish all the time. I absolutely loved it and learnt how to cook it myself as soon as I was old enough. I used to eat this with creamy mashed potato. I would make a well in the centre of my mashed potato and spoon in the meat juices. Add mushy peas to make this an even more delicious and warming meal.

Put the olive oil in a large stockpot and place over medium heat. Add the girello and cook for about 10 minutes, turning the meat around in the pot every few minutes, until it browns on all sides. The meat and the base of the pot should be dark brown (but not charcoal) in colour from the meat juices.

Once the meat has browned, add the onion and garlic and cook for a further 4 minutes. Add the stock cube, bay leaves, cloves, salt and pepper. Add enough water to fill about three-quarters of the stockpot and completely cover the meat.

Simmer, covered, over medium heat for about 1 hour and 45 minutes, or until the meat is meltingly tender. (Check to see how the water level is going every 30 minutes. If the water has reduced a lot, add another ½ cup.)

After 1 hour, turn the meat over. Taste the juice to see if the dish needs any additional salt and adjust accordingly.

At the end of the cooking time, there should be about 5 cm of juice left in the stockpot. Check to see this is the case. If not, continue cooking until you have this much juice.

When ready, remove the girello from the stockpot using long-handled tongs and place on a chopping board. Using a sharp knife and holding the meat steady with the tongs, slice the meat into 1 cm thick slices.

Using a large slotted spoon, remove the bay leaves and cloves from the pot. Place the sliced meat back in the stockpot and place over medium heat until the sauce comes to the boil.

Place 2 slices of meat on each of four serving plates and drizzle with a little sauce. Serve alongside a generous dollop of creamy mashed potato and some baby spinach leaves.

mmm ... mushy peas please

Butter chicken

India

Medium

6

Serves

There aren't enough words to describe how delicious this dish really is. I usually eat butter chicken with Coconut Rice (see page 73) and pappadums to make a complete meal out of it.

To make the garam masala, place all of the spices in a heavy-based frying pan over low heat. Stir for 1 minute with a wooden spoon, or until the spices become aromatic (this is called 'dry-roasting'). Remove from the heat as soon as the spices become fragrant and set aside in a small bowl.

Place the onion, garlic, lemon juice, ginger, salt, garam masala and 1 tablespoon of the olive oil in a food processor. Blitz to form a paste (for extra information on how to do this, see page 113).

Put the remaining oil in a frying pan and place over low heat. Add the chicken and lightly cook for 2 minutes on each side. Remove the chicken and set aside.

Add the butter and onion paste to the frying pan and cook, stirring occasionally, over low heat for 3–4 minutes, or until the onion is soft and translucent.

As the onion paste cooks, add the sugar and 1 cup of warm water to a measuring jug. Use a whisk to gently combine. Add this liquid to the frying pan and stir well. Simmer for 10 minutes over low–medium heat.

Return the chicken to the frying pan. Cover with a lid and cook over low heat for 10 minutes, or until the chicken is just cooked through.

Spoon the chicken and sauce into a large dish and serve with Coconut Rice (see page 73) and pappadums.

GARAM MASALA*

¼ teaspoon **ground cumin**

¼ teaspoon **ground fennel**

¼ teaspoon **ground cardamom**

¼ teaspoon **ground cinnamon**

¼ teaspoon **ground nutmeg**

1 **onion**, halved

4 **garlic cloves**, peeled

1 tablespoon **lemon juice**

knob of **ginger**, about 5 cm x 2 cm, peeled

1 teaspoon **salt**

2 tablespoons **olive oil**

3 free-range **chicken breast fillets** (about 750 g in total), cut into 3 cm cubes

50 g **butter**

1 tablespoon **sugar**

EQUIPMENT

measuring spoons

heavy-based frying pan with lid

wooden spoon

small mixing bowl

food processor

tongs

measuring cups

measuring jug

whisk

Did you know that many Indians eat with their right hand only? They use breads such as naan and chapati to help scoop up the food.

Sides

Perfect fries

500 g floury **potatoes**

2 cups **vegetable oil**,
for deep-frying

2 pinches of **salt**

tomato sauce (ketchup),
to serve

EQUIPMENT

2 baking trays
paper towel
peeler
tea towel
chopping board
sharp knife
medium mixing bowl
measuring cups
large saucepan or deep-fryer
slotted spoon
tongs

USA

Medium

4

Serves

When you visit your local greengrocer ask them for non-waxy potatoes with a floury texture and low moisture content. Sounds like quite a mouthful, but honestly, this is one of the secrets to making the perfect potato fry. Some great varieties to use are sebago, russet burbank, bintje or spunta. If you want to be a bit healthier, slice your fries thicker – a thicker fry will absorb less oil!

Line two baking trays with paper towel.

Carefully peel the potatoes away from your body. Wash them well under cool water and dry them completely.

Cut the potatoes lengthways into ½ cm wide slices. Cut each slice lengthways again into ½ cm wide fries. Pat the fries dry with paper towel (this helps to prevent the oil splattering during the cooking process) and put them in a bowl.

Pour the oil into a large saucepan or deep-fryer and place over high heat for about 7 minutes. Next, test to see if the oil is hot enough by carefully placing a chip into it. If the chip bubbles away ferociously the oil is hot enough.

When the oil is ready, carefully put all of the fries into the saucepan using a slotted spoon. Partially cook, turning once, for about 8 minutes, or until they are just golden and tender but not browned.

Using a slotted spoon, remove the fries and place on the baking tray. Set aside.

Reheat the same oil on high for a further 2 minutes, or until a test chip bubbles away when placed in the oil.

Using the slotted spoon, place the partially cooked fries back into the oil, being careful not to bring any paper with them. Cook for another 30 seconds to 1 minute, or until crisp and golden, separating any fries that stick together. Be prepared to start removing fries from the oil soon after you start re-frying them, as they go from golden to dark brown very quickly.

Using tongs, carefully transfer the fries onto a serving dish. Scatter over the salt and toss to combine. Serve straight away with a small dish of tomato sauce.

Did you know that Americans call tomato sauce ketchup? It was first produced and sold to the public by Heinz in 1876.

Cheese and herb damper

This damper is based on a basic scone recipe — it doesn't use yeast, so doesn't need to prove (rise) before it is baked. It is best eaten straight from the oven and is great served with a smear of butter or dipped into a hearty soup!

Preheat the oven to 170°C (Gas 3). Grease a baking tray with the butter, using some scrunched-up baking paper.

Crumble the feta into a mixing bowl. Add the cheddar cheese and herbs and mix well.

Sift the flour into a second mixing bowl. Set aside.

Combine the milk, cream and lemon juice in a measuring jug. Add this to the cheese mix and stir well.

Add the milk and cheese mix to the flour and mix well with your hands (for more information on how to knead dough, see page 113). The dough should be very soft and just hold its shape. Do not overwork the dough or your damper will end up hard.

Dust the bench with a little extra flour then turn the dough out onto the bench. Generously flour your hands, then divide the dough into nine even-sized balls.

Arrange the balls on the baking tray so that there are three rows of three balls. Place the balls close enough together to be touching each other. Brush the extra milk over the damper with a pastry brush.

Place the damper on the middle shelf of the oven and cook for 20 minutes, or until risen and golden. Wearing oven mitts, carefully remove the damper from the oven. Allow to cool for 5 minutes before removing from the tray with an egg flip and serving. The inside of the damper will be a bit doughy but that's as it should be!

Australia

Medium

9

Makes

1 tablespoon **butter**, for greasing

80 g **feta cheese**

1 cup grated **cheddar cheese**

4 **parsley sprigs**, finely chopped

10 **chives**, finely snipped

2 cups **self-raising flour**

200 ml **milk**

200 ml **thickened cream**

½ teaspoon **lemon juice**

plain flour, for dusting

2 tablespoons **milk**, extra

EQUIPMENT

measuring spoons

baking tray

baking paper

medium mixing bowls

grater

measuring cups

large metal spoon

sifter

measuring jug

pastry brush

oven mitts

egg flip

Damper was originally cooked on campfires by stockmen who worked in the Australian outback and had only basic cooking supplies.

Scalloped potatoes

300 ml **thickened cream**
½ cup grated **cheddar cheese**
1 teaspoon **salt**
2 pinches of **black pepper**
½ teaspoon **ground nutmeg**
1 kg small, floury **potatoes**,
such as desiree

EQUIPMENT
measuring jug
grater
measuring cups
measuring spoons
medium mixing bowl
large metal spoon
peeler
tea towel
chopping board
sharp knife
ceramic baking dish,
30 cm x 22 cm x 5 cm high
ladle
foil
oven mitts

UK

Medium

Serves

This is a delicious side dish that is great served with roast meats or even grilled or pan-fried fish. You can prepare the dish ahead of time and keep it in the fridge for up to half a day. When you're ready, just place it in the oven and cook as instructed. Some heartier versions of scalloped potatoes include crispy bacon, onions, breadcrumbs and herbs. This isn't something I recommend you eat all the time though as it's quite heavy and rich.

Preheat the oven to 180°C (Gas 4).

Place the cream, cheese, salt, pepper and nutmeg in a bowl. Mix well and set aside.

Peel, wash and dry the potatoes, remembering to peel away from yourself. Slice the potatoes into ½ cm thick rounds.

Layer half of the potatoes evenly across the bottom of a baking dish. Ladle over half of the cream mixture. Repeat with the remainder of the potatoes and cream mixture.

Cover the baking dish with foil. Place the dish on the middle shelf of the oven and bake for 45 minutes to 1 hour, or until the potatoes are just tender.

Carefully remove the foil from the baking dish wearing oven mitts. Cook, uncovered, for a further 15 minutes, or until the top is crisp and golden.

Wearing oven mitts, remove the baking dish from the oven and serve immediately.

If you want to make these scalloped potatoes a little bit healthier, you can replace half of the cream with beef or chicken stock.

Fresh guacamole

Mexico

Easy

Serves

Guacamole, or avocado dip, makes a wonderful, fresh accompaniment to Frijole Nachos (see page 28). It's so easy to make that there really is no excuse for buying the store-bought versions, which don't compare taste-wise to the real thing. You can even spread a little guacamole in a sandwich with shredded roast chicken for your lunch!

Place the onion in a food processor and blitz to a paste (for extra information on how to do this, see page 113).

Slice the avocado in half lengthways and remove the stone. Scoop out the avocado flesh into the food processor with the onion, being sure not to include any flesh that is grey, black or brown. Squeeze in the lemon juice and add the salt and pepper.

Blitz on high for 1 minute, or until the dip is smooth and creamy. Using a spatula, scrape down the sides of the processor as you go, making sure the avocado is mixed in properly.

Remove the lid and blade from the processor. Scoop the guacamole out into a serving bowl and sprinkle with the spring onions and paprika if using. Serve straight away, as fresh guacamole discolours if left to sit for too long!

¼ small **onion**

1 ripe **avocado**

juice of ½ **lemon**

½ teaspoon **salt**

1 pinch of **black pepper**

1 **spring onion** (optional), thinly sliced

2 pinches of **sweet paprika** (optional)

EQUIPMENT

food processor

spatula

chopping board

sharp knife

measuring spoons

spatula

metal tablespoon

Coconut rice

Thailand

Easy

4 Serves

1¼ cups **jasmine rice***
1 x 400 g can of **coconut milk**
2 tablespoons **sugar**
1 tablespoon **coconut oil**
(optional)
2 tablespoons **toasted shredded coconut**, to garnish

EQUIPMENT
measuring cups
rice cooker
measuring spoons
wooden spoon
fork

The first time I made coconut rice I was surprised at how easy it was to prepare. I automatically thought something that tasted so good must have required a lot of effort ... how wrong I was! Serve this alongside any Thai curry as a delicious accompaniment to soak up all the sauce. This version calls for the use of a rice cooker – please use metric measuring cups and not the cup that comes with your rice cooker to make sure you get the right results!

Put the rice in the rice cooker. Add 1 cup of water, along with the coconut milk and sugar. Stir well with a wooden spoon.

Cover the cooker with a lid and set to 'cook' mode. (As a guide, my cooker takes about 25 minutes to cook this amount of rice.) Once the cooker switches to 'warm' mode, allow it to rest for another 5 minutes, so the rice finishes softening.

When ready, add the coconut oil, if using, and fluff up the rice with a fork.

Transfer the rice to small bowls and serve straight away, garnished with the toasted coconut.

Did you know that the shape of Thailand is similar to the profile of an elephant with its long trunk stretching down the peninsula?

73

Potato gems

Japan

Medium

15

Makes

I've put a Japanese-inspired twist on regular, crispy potato gems with the addition of sesame seeds and soy sauce (shoyu) for dipping. These would be perfect served at your next birthday party celebration! If you're not keen on soy sauce, these gems are also delicious served alongside some good-quality mayonnaise.

Grease a baking tray with the butter, using some scrunched-up baking paper.

Peel, wash and dry the potatoes, remembering to peel away from yourself. If the potatoes are large, use a sharp knife to slice them in half. Set aside.

Fill a saucepan with boiling water and place over high heat until it reaches a rolling boil (see page 112 for more information on the different ways you can boil something). Using a slotted spoon, carefully lower the potatoes into the water. Boil the potatoes for 15 minutes, or until just tender. Use the slotted spoon to drain the potatoes and place them on a chopping board to cool.

Place the onion in a food processor and blitz to a paste (for extra information on how to do this, see page 113). Transfer to a mixing bowl. Add the egg, breadcrumbs, salt and pepper and combine well.

When the potatoes have completely cooled, coarsely grate them on the chopping board. Add to the egg and breadcrumb mixture and combine well.

Take 1 tablespoon of the mix and, using your hands, roll into a small, round gem and place on the baking tray. Continue rolling gems until all the mixture has been used up.

Next, put the sesame seeds in a small bowl. Coat the gems in the sesame seeds one at a time and return them to the tray.

Put the oil in a wok and place over high heat for 5 minutes, or until a tiny piece of potato bubbles away when placed in the oil. When ready, carefully place half of the gems in the wok using tongs, being careful to not get splashed by the oil.

Fry the gems for about 1½ minutes on each side, or until they are golden brown. Remove the gems using tongs and drain well on paper towel. Repeat this process for the remainder of the gems.

Arrange the gems on a platter and serve immediately alongside a small bowl of soy sauce.

1 teaspoon **butter**, for greasing

300 g **potatoes** (sebago or coliban are best)

1 **onion**, halved

1 **egg**, beaten well

¼ cup **breadcrumbs**

1 teaspoon **salt**

2 pinches of **black pepper**

⅓ cup **white sesame seeds**

3 cups **vegetable oil**

soy sauce, to serve

EQUIPMENT

baking tray

baking paper

peeler

tea towel

sharp knife

chopping board

medium saucepan

slotted spoon

food processor

large metal spoon

large mixing bowl

measuring cups

measuring spoons

grater

small bowl

wok

tongs

paper towel

Biscuits & Cakes

uno due tre

Mum's lemon biscotti

1 tablespoon **butter**, for greasing
130 g **unsalted butter**
2½ cups **self-raising flour**
150 g **sour cream**
1 **egg**
1 **egg yolk**
1 teaspoon grated **lemon zest**
1 cup **caster sugar**
1 teaspoon **vanilla extract**
¼ teaspoon **bicarbonate of soda**
½ cup **icing sugar**

EQUIPMENT
baking trays
baking paper
small saucepan
measuring jug
measuring spoons
measuring cups
zester or grater
large mixing bowl
wooden spoon
plastic wrap
large plate
oven mitts
egg flip
wire racks

Italy

Easy

35

Makes

My mum taught me how to make these biscuits. They were passed down from a friend of a friend. They're kind of chewy on the outside and soft on the inside, and they're so easy to make. You must be patient and let the dough rest in the fridge for at least 20 minutes before rolling, otherwise it will be too soft to roll out properly before cooking.

Preheat the oven to 200°C (Gas 6). Grease three baking trays with the tablespoon of butter, using some scrunched-up baking paper.

Put the unsalted butter in a small saucepan and melt over medium heat. Set aside.

Combine the remaining ingredients, except the icing sugar, in a large mixing bowl, then pour in the butter. Mix well with a wooden spoon – you should get a firm dough. Cover the bowl with plastic wrap and refrigerate for at least 20 minutes.

Remove the dough from the fridge and roll tablespoons of it into balls. When you have used all of the dough, spread the icing sugar onto a large plate and roll the balls, a few at a time, in the sugar so that they are generously coated. Place 5 cm apart on the baking trays.

Bake the biscuits on the middle and bottom shelves of the oven for 8–10 minutes, or until just lightly golden.

Carefully remove the trays from the oven using oven mitts. Cool for a couple of minutes, then remove the biscuits from the trays with an egg flip and place them on wire racks to cool completely.

While the word 'biscuit' is actually French in origin, 'biscotti' is the Italian plural word to describe 'many biscuits'!

79

Chai tea cupcakes

India

Easy

15
Makes

This is an Indian-inspired sweet treat. I'm pretty sure cupcakes aren't traditionally enjoyed in India, but I do know that chai tea is! I've combined the best of both worlds to give you these delicious cupcakes.

Preheat the oven to 180°C (Gas 4). Line cupcake tins with 15 patty cases.

Place the milk and chai tea in a small saucepan over medium heat and stir well with a wooden spoon. Bring to the boil, then remove from the heat and strain into a small bowl. Discard the tea.

Place the butter, sugar and vanilla in a large bowl. Using an electric mixer, beat on high for about 3 minutes, or until light and fluffy. Add the eggs and beat well, scraping down the sides of the bowl with a spatula a few times.

Add the flour, spices, baking powder and strained milk. Beat on medium speed until well combined. The mixture will be very thick and creamy.

Evenly spoon the batter into the patty cases with a metal tablespoon, filling them nearly to the top. Try to smooth the top as best you can.

Bake on the middle shelf of the oven for 15–20 minutes, or until a skewer inserted into the centre of the cupcakes comes out clean.

Remove the cupcakes from the oven using oven mitts. Take them out of the tin and place them on a wire rack. If you like, you can leave the cupcakes to cool completely, then ice them with Chocolate Buttercream Frosting (see page 84).

If you'd prefer, you could just lightly dust the top of the cupcakes with icing sugar instead of using Chocolate Buttercream Frosting.

1 cup **milk**

½ cup loose-leaf **chai tea**

200 g **butter**, softened

1¼ cups **brown sugar**

1 tablespoon **vanilla extract**

2 **eggs**

2 cups **plain flour**

2 teaspoons **ground cinnamon**

1 teaspoon **ground ginger**

1 teaspoon **ground cardamom**

1 teaspoon **ground cloves**

½ teaspoon freshly grated **nutmeg** (or 1 teaspoon **ground nutmeg**)

1 teaspoon **baking powder**

Chocolate Buttercream Frosting (optional), see page 84

EQUIPMENT

cupcake tins

patty cases

measuring cups

small saucepan

wooden spoon

strainer

small mixing bowl

measuring spoons

large mixing bowl

electric mixer

spatula

zester or grater

metal tablespoon

skewer

oven mitts

wire rack

Lamingtons

1 tablespoon **butter**, for greasing
1 tablespoon **plain flour**
130 g **cornflour**
1 teaspoon **baking powder**
4 **eggs**, separated
¾ cup **caster sugar**
3 cups **desiccated coconut**

CHOCOLATE ICING
2½ cups **icing sugar**
20 g **rich cocoa**
½ cup **boiling water**

EQUIPMENT
2 loaf tins, 26 cm x 11 cm
baking paper
measuring spoons
sifter
medium mixing bowls
electric mixer
measuring cups
spatula
large metal spoon
skewer
oven mitts
palette knife
wire rack
large chopping board
sharp knife
whisk
large plate
tongs

Australia

Tricky

24

Makes

When I was in primary school we used to sell lamingtons to raise money for the school each year. I have fond memories of this event, but I must admit that my homemade lamingtons are much better than the store-bought ones we used to sell from school!

Preheat the oven to 170°C (Gas 3). Grease two loaf tins, each 26 cm x 11 cm, with the butter, using some scrunched-up baking paper, then dust with the plain four.

Sift the cornflour and baking powder into a medium bowl. Set aside.

Put the egg whites in a clean, dry bowl. Using an electric mixer, beat the egg whites on high for about 20 seconds, or until foamy. Add the sugar and beat for about 5 minutes, or until thick and glossy. You'll need to stop halfway through this process to scrape down the sides of the bowl with a spatula. Next, mix in the egg yolks. Finally, fold in the cornflour and baking powder using a metal spoon.

Spoon the mixture into the loaf tins and bake on the middle shelf of the oven for 25 minutes, or until a skewer inserted into the centre of the cakes comes out clean.

Remove the cakes from the oven using oven mitts and allow to cool for 5 minutes.

Use a palette knife to cut around the cakes, then remove them from their tins by inverting them (tipping them upside down on the bench). Place the cakes on a wire rack to cool completely.

Place the cakes on a large chopping board. Using a sharp knife, slice each cake in half lengthways. Next, slice the halves widthways into six strips. Square off your cake edges on all sides if desired.

To make the chocolate icing, sift the icing sugar and cocoa into a bowl. Carefully pour in the boiling water and whisk until smooth. Spread the coconut out on a large plate.

Place two pieces of cake into the icing. Use tongs to evenly coat the cake pieces on all sides, then remove and allow any excess icing to drip off into the bowl.

Transfer the iced pieces into the coconut and use your fingers to evenly coat the lamingtons on all sides, then transfer to a wire rack. Repeat the process until all the lamingtons are made.

Leave the lamingtons for at least 3 hours on the bench (not in the fridge) to allow the icing to set before eating.

seriously yummy

Devil's food cake

USA

Easy

10-12

Serves

This cake has its origins in the south of the USA and is similar to red velvet cake. If you like, you could add ¼–½ cup of smooth peanut butter to the frosting.

Preheat the oven to 170°C (Gas 3). Grease two cake tins, each 20 cm round, with the butter, using some scrunched-up baking paper, then dust with the plain four.

Half fill a medium saucepan with boiling water and place over medium heat. Put the chocolate into a small saucepan, then position it on top of the medium saucepan, making sure that the water isn't touching the bottom of the small saucepan. Melt the chocolate, stirring occasionally with a wooden spoon, until completely smooth. Carefully remove the small saucepan from the heat and allow to cool.

Sift the self-raising flour, cocoa, baking powder and salt into a large bowl.

Place the sugar, vanilla, milk, eggs, oil and melted chocolate in another large bowl and beat with an electric mixer until smooth. Add the flour and cocoa mixture and beat on high for about 1 minute, or until just combined.

Use a spatula to scrape the batter into the tins, making sure that you evenly distribute half the batter into each tin. Bake on the middle and lower shelves of the oven for 25 minutes, or until a skewer inserted into the centre of the cakes comes out clean.

Remove the cakes from the oven using oven mitts. Cut all the way around the cakes with a palette knife and leave to cool in the tins for 10 minutes. Carefully turn the cakes out onto wire racks. Cool for at least 30 minutes before icing.

To make the frosting, half fill a medium saucepan with boiling water and place over medium heat. Place the milk chocolate and dark chocolate into a small saucepan, then position it on top of the medium saucepan, making sure that the water isn't touching the bottom of the small saucepan. Melt the chocolate, stirring occasionally, until completely smooth. Carefully remove the small saucepan from the heat and allow to cool.

Combine the butter, milk, cocoa, icing sugar and vanilla in a bowl. Using an electric mixer, beat on high for about 5 minutes, or until light and fluffy.

Add the cooled melted chocolate and beat again on high for about 1 minute, or until light and fluffy. Be careful not to over-beat the frosting – the longer you beat the mixture, the thicker the frosting will be, and this will make it difficult to spread.

Place one of the cakes on a serving plate. Using a spatula, heap one-third of the frosting on top and start smoothing it all the way around the top until the cake is completely covered.

Place the other cake directly on top of the iced cake. Completely cover the double-layer cake with frosting, making sure the sides and top are covered. You may like to create decorative swirls on the icing using your palette knife.

2 tablespoons **butter**

2 tablespoons **plain flour**

200 g **milk chocolate**, roughly chopped

2 cups **self-raising flour**

½ cup rich **cocoa**

1 teaspoon **baking powder**

½ teaspoon **salt**

2 cups **caster sugar**

1 tablespoon **vanilla extract**

½ cup **milk**

4 **eggs**

½ cup **vegetable oil**

CHOCOLATE BUTTERCREAM FROSTING

100 g **milk chocolate**, roughly chopped

100 g **dark chocolate**, roughly chopped

100 g **unsalted butter**, softened

1½ tablespoons **milk**

2 tablespoons rich **cocoa**

1 cup **icing sugar**

1 tablespoon **vanilla extract**

EQUIPMENT

2 cake tins, 20 cm round

baking paper

measuring spoons

medium saucepan

small saucepan

wooden spoon

large mixing bowls

measuring cups

sifter

electric mixer

spatula

skewer

oven mitts

palette knives

wire racks

Green tea cupcakes with lime glaze

⅓ cup **green tea leaves** or 5 **green tea bags**

300 ml **boiling water**

300 g **butter**, roughly chopped and softened

1½ cups **caster sugar**

6 **eggs**

2⅓ cups **self-raising flour**

LIME GLAZE

1 cup **icing sugar**

¼ cup **boiling water**

grated zest from ½ **lime**

1 tablespoon **lime juice**

EQUIPMENT

cupcake tins

patty cases

measuring jug

strainer

small mixing bowls

metal spoon

electric mixer

measuring cups

large mixing bowl

large metal spoons

skewer

oven mitts

wire rack

zester or grater

whisk

This recipe puts a Western spin on a famous Japanese ingredient – sencha, commonly known as green tea. You could make the glaze for these cupcakes using strained green tea mixed with icing sugar, but I really like the zing that lime juice adds!

Preheat the oven to 170°C (Gas 3). Line cupcake tins with 20 patty cases.

Place the tea leaves or bags in a measuring jug with the boiling water and steep (or sit) for 10 minutes. Sieve the tea through a strainer into a small bowl, pressing out any excess moisture with a spoon. Discard the tea leaves or bags.

Using an electric mixer, cream the butter and sugar in a large bowl on high for 3 minutes, or until light and creamy. Add the eggs one at a time, beating well after each addition. Sift in the flour, then pour in the green tea and beat until the batter is smooth.

Carefully spoon the batter into the patty cases using a large metal spoon so that it reaches three-quarters of the way up the side. Make sure there are no air pockets.

Bake on the middle and lower shelves of the oven for 20 minutes, or until a skewer inserted into the centre of the cakes comes out clean.

Remove the tins from the oven using oven mitts, then remove the cakes and place on a wire rack to cool.

To make the glaze, combine the icing sugar and boiling water in a small bowl. Add the lime zest and juice and whisk until well combined.

Once the cakes are cool, transfer them to a large serving platter and drizzle over the icing.

It's best to allow the glaze to set a bit before eating these cakes, as they can get quite messy!

Almond crescent biscuits

Greece

Easy

18 Makes

These biscuits are highly addictive – beware, you'll be a convert as soon as you taste one! They are delicious served with a pot of chamomile for afternoon tea.

Preheat the oven to 160°C (Gas 2–3). Grease a baking tray with the butter, using some scrunched-up baking paper.

Combine the almond meal and sugar in a large bowl and mix well with a large metal spoon. Set aside.

Using an electric mixer, beat the egg whites in a clean bowl on high for 2 minutes, or until they are stiff. Add the egg whites to the almond meal and sugar. Gently stir until the mixture just forms a firm paste. Do not overmix, or your biscuits will turn out hard!

Working on the bench, roll tablespoons of the biscuit paste into 7 cm long rolls. Repeat until all the mixture is used.

Smooth the ends of each roll, then shape into crescents (half moons). Place the biscuits 3 cm apart on the baking tray.

Bake the biscuits for 10 minutes only on the middle shelf of the oven. The biscuits will come out pale and very soft – that's perfect! (If you overcook these biscuits they will end up very hard.)

Remove the tray from the oven using oven mitts. Cool for a couple of minutes, then remove the biscuits from the tray with an egg flip and place them on wire racks to cool completely.

Before serving, use a sifter to lightly dust the biscuits with the icing sugar.

1 teaspoon **butter**, for greasing
2 cups **almond meal**
¾ cup **caster sugar**
2 **egg whites**
¼ cup **icing sugar**, for dusting

EQUIPMENT
baking tray
baking paper
measuring spoons
measuring cups
large bowl
large metal spoon
electric mixer
medium bowl
oven mitts
egg flip
wire racks
sifter

Use your leftover yolks from this recipe to make French toast! Place the egg yolks in a bowl. Add ½ cup milk (and either a little salt or sugar) and whisk well. Dip a few slices of bread into this mixture and fry in a little butter or vegetable oil over medium heat for 2–3 minutes on each side, or until golden.

Valencia orange cake

2–3 large valencia **oranges** (approximately 650 g in total)
1 teaspoon **butter**
6 **eggs**
1½ cups **caster sugar**
1½ teaspoons **baking powder**
2 cups **almond meal**
¾ cup **self-raising flour**
1½ tablespoons **icing sugar**
whipped cream, to serve

EQUIPMENT
saucepan with lid
skewer
tongs
chopping board
22 cm springform cake tin
measuring spoons
baking paper
whisk
measuring cups
large mixing bowl
large metal spoon
sharp knife
food processor
oven mitts
wire rack
sifter

Spain
Medium

Serves

Orange cake hails from a town in Spain called Valencia. Valencia is well known for lending its name to a type of orange variety grown there. Having said that, you don't need to use valencia oranges for this recipe if you don't have them. Navel or other varieties will be just fine! I recommend using organic oranges as you won't be peeling them but using the whole orange, skin and all.

Place the oranges in a saucepan with enough boiling water to cover them and cover with a lid. The oranges will float, but should be mostly covered. Simmer over medium heat for 45 minutes, or until a skewer slides easily through the oranges. Remove them from the saucepan using tongs and place on a chopping board to cool.

Preheat the oven to 180°C (Gas 4). Grease a 22 cm springform cake tin with the butter, using some scrunched-up baking paper. Place the cake tin on a sheet of baking paper and draw a circle around the tin. Cut out the circle and position it in the base of the tin, sticking it down well.

Whisk the eggs and sugar in a large bowl for 3 minutes, or until light and creamy. Add the baking powder and almond meal and mix well with a large metal spoon. Set aside.

Once the oranges have cooled enough to safely touch them, use a sharp knife to slice each one in half and remove the pips, pith (interior white part) and stem nub.

Transfer the oranges to a food processor and blitz until you have a smooth paste without big lumps. Be careful as the steam from the oranges may cause the processor lid to pop off unexpectedly. It's a good idea to firmly press your hand down on the lid as you process.

Add the orange paste to the cake batter and mix thoroughly. Pour into the cake tin and bake on the middle shelf of the oven for 40 minutes, or until a skewer inserted into the centre of the cake comes out clean.

Remove the cake from the oven using oven mitts and cool in the tin for 10 minutes. Then remove the springform tin and place the cake on a wire rack to cool completely.

Sift the icing sugar over the cake and serve with a dollop of whipped cream.

In terms of holiday destinations, Spain is the third most visited country in the world!

Desserts

grated orange zest · HEAVY-BASED SAUCEPAN · ¾ SIFTER · ½ cup boiling water · MAKE THE DAY BEFORE · drizzling the milk · MEASURE · UFF PASTRY · WOODEN SPOON · RAMEKIN · 1 LITRE OF MILK · whisking quickly · electric mixer · WHISK · SQUEEZE LEMON JUICE · MELT BUTTER · TONGS · cinnamon quills · CRYSTALLISE · plastic wrap · CASTER SUGAR · CUP · 180°C · SMALL RAMEKINS · DRIZZLE · mix · MEASURING JUG · beat the eggs · ORANGE BLOSSOM · SCISSORS · whipped cream · BLUNT KNIFE · beat the eggs and remaining sugar · 30 SECONDS · spoon · custard is set · 1 teaspoon · ¼ TEASPOON GROUND CINNAMON · OVEN MITTS · DUST WITH ICING SUGAR · CRÈME CARAMELS · 1 TEASPOON GRATED ORANGE ZEST

Orange blossom and cinnamon rice pudding

Morocco

Easy

4
Serves

This is a Moroccan spin on a usually very English dessert! It's important to use good-quality risotto rice for this recipe, not just a cheap arborio from the supermarket. If you use the right kind of rice, the end result will be beautifully rich without being gluggy. It's also very important not to wash the rice first. If you do you'll remove all the starch, which is what makes the rice pudding rich and creamy!

Place the milk, sugar, cinnamon quills and orange zest in a small saucepan over low heat. Bring to a simmer, stirring with a wooden spoon to help dissolve the sugar. Remove from the heat.

Place the rice and one ladle-ful of the warmed milk in a large saucepan over low–medium heat. Stir with a wooden spoon until all the milk is absorbed. Continue to add the milk, ¾ cup at a time, until all the milk has been used up and your rice is 'al dente' (for tips on how to check if something is 'al dente', see page 113). Make sure that each ladle of milk is fully absorbed before adding the next.

Remove the saucepan from the heat and add the orange blossom water. Use some tongs to remove the cinnamon quills, then stir the rice for another 30 seconds.

Spoon an even amount of rice pudding into four serving bowls. Sprinkle with the ground cinnamon and serve straight away.

1 litre **milk**

¼–⅓ cup **caster sugar**

2 **cinnamon quills**

1 teaspoon grated **orange zest**

½ cup **vialone nano rice***

3 teaspoons **orange blossom water***

½ teaspoon **ground cinnamon**

EQUIPMENT

measuring jug

measuring cups

measuring spoons

zester or grater

small saucepan

wooden spoon

ladle

large heavy-based saucepan

tongs

The final 30-second stir of the rice is called 'mantecato' in Italian and will make this dish extra rich and creamy!

Crispy coconut bananas

Thailand

Easy

4
Serves

8 very firm **ladyfinger bananas**
¾ cup **cornflour**
¾ cup **plain flour** or
potato flour*
½ teaspoon **baking powder**
2 tablespoons **caster sugar**
1 teaspoon **salt**
2 teaspoons **vanilla extract**
½ cup **shredded coconut**
¾ cup **soda** or **mineral water**
2 tablespoons **boiling water**
3 cups **vegetable oil**
2 tablespoons **icing sugar**
vanilla ice-cream (optional),
to serve

EQUIPMENT
baking tray
paper towel
sharp knife
chopping board
medium mixing bowl
measuring cups
measuring spoons
large metal spoon
wok or large frying pan
tongs
sifter

This recipe can be messy to prepare, but once cooked, it looks and tastes amazing. It's quite a basic recipe to master, so do try it early on in your cooking endeavours. Enjoy these bananas on their own or on top of some pancakes and drizzled with maple syrup.

Line a baking tray with some paper towel.

Peel the bananas, then slice each one lengthways on a chopping board, following the curve of the banana.

In a mixing bowl, combine the flours, baking powder, sugar, salt, vanilla and coconut. Add the soda water and boiling water. Mix well to form a thick batter.

Put the oil in a wok or large frying pan and place over high heat for 5 minutes, or until a tiny dollop of batter bubbles away when you drop it in.

Using your fingers, dip each piece of banana into the batter to completely coat. Using tongs, carefully place four pieces of banana at a time into the oil. Fry for 1½–2 minutes on each side, or until golden.

Use the tongs to remove the bananas from the oil and drain on the paper towel. Repeat this process until all of the pieces have been cooked.

Arrange the bananas on dessert plates. Sift over the icing sugar and serve alongside some vanilla ice-cream, if desired.

a-roi maak maak

Crème caramel

France

Tricky

6
Serves

The first time I made crème caramel was when I was 8, under my mum's watchful eye. This is the French version, although Puerto Ricans and Catalans make a similar dessert. It is best made a day ahead as it needs to set.

Preheat the oven to 160°C (Gas 2–3). Arrange six small ramekins in a large roasting dish.

Place the boiling water and 1½ cups of the sugar in a small heavy-based saucepan and mix well with a wooden spoon to dissolve some of the sugar. Place the saucepan over low heat for 4 minutes, or until all the sugar has dissolved. Do not stir! Also, don't be tempted to swirl the caramel around the pan as this will make it crystallise (or go grainy).

Turn the heat up to medium and allow the mixture to boil (without stirring) for 4 minutes, or until the caramel changes from light gold to a slightly darker shade of brown. Don't walk away as the caramel can change from golden to bitter and unusable in the blink of an eye!

Remove the caramel from the heat and evenly ladle it into the ramekins. As you do this, the caramel will darken slightly – don't worry, this is normal. Set aside.

Using an electric mixer, beat the eggs and remaining ½ cup of sugar in a medium bowl on high for about 1 minute, or until light and frothy. Set aside.

Place the milk, cream and vanilla into a medium saucepan over medium heat, whisking occasionally, for about 6 minutes, or until just simmering. Ask an adult to very slowly drizzle the warmed milk into the egg mixture while you quickly whisk (this will ensure that the eggs don't cook from the heat).

Position a sieve over a mixing bowl and pour the custard through the sieve. Allow to cool for 10 minutes, then pour the custard into the ramekins (over the set caramel). Carefully pour enough boiling water into the roasting dish to reach halfway up the side of each ramekin.

Cook the crème caramels on the middle shelf of the oven for 25–30 minutes, or until the custard is just set. The custard should be bouncy but not liquidy to touch.

Carefully remove the roasting dish from the oven using oven mitts and transfer the ramekins onto a baking tray using tongs. Leave to cool for 1 hour, then cover each ramekin with plastic wrap and place in the fridge for at least 7 hours, or until set.

When ready to serve, remove the plastic wrap and run a blunt knife around the inner edge of each ramekin. Position a dessert plate over the top of the ramekin. Use one hand to firmly press down on the plate as you lift the ramekin up off the bench. In a quick motion, tip the plate and ramekin upside down, making sure they're still in firm contact with each other.

Hold the plate and ramekin together (with the plate the right side up) and vigorously shake the crème caramel out of its ramekin. You should be able to hear it slide out! Allow all of the caramel to drip out from the ramekin and onto the crème caramel.

Repeat for the other crème caramels. Serve with some whipped cream on the side, if desired.

¼ cup **boiling water**

2 cups **caster sugar**

6 **eggs**

1 cup **milk**

1 cup **thickened cream**

2 tablespoons **vanilla extract**

whipped cream (optional),
to serve

EQUIPMENT

6 small ramekins, about
¾ cup capacity

large roasting dish

measuring cups

small, heavy-based saucepan

wooden spoon

ladles

electric mixer

medium mixing bowls

measuring spoons

medium saucepan

whisk

sieve

oven mitts

baking tray

tongs

plastic wrap

blunt knife

France's capital city, Paris, is one of the most visited places in the world. Its most famous tourist attractions include the Eiffel Tower, the Louvre and Notre Dame Cathedral.

Mini pavlovas with passionfruit curd

Australia

Tricky

8 Makes

6 **egg whites**
¾ teaspoon **cream of tartar***
2 teaspoons **vanilla extract**
1¼ cups **caster sugar**
2 tablespoons **cornflour**
1½ teaspoons **white vinegar**
600 ml **cream**, lightly whipped
pulp of 4 **passionfruit**
3 small **bananas**, thinly sliced

PASSIONFRUIT CURD

⅓ cup **passionfruit pulp** (you'll need 6–8 passionfruit)
1½ tablespoons **lemon juice**
90 g **butter**, roughly chopped
¼ cup **caster sugar**
3 **egg yolks**

EQUIPMENT

large mixing bowl
measuring spoons
electric mixer
measuring cups
baking trays
baking paper
large metal spoon
oven mitts
small saucepan
wooden spoon
whisk
medium mixing bowl
small bowl

Nothing beats a homemade pavlova! You can make the meringue with either caster sugar or icing sugar – caster sugar helps to form a hard crust on the outside of the pavlova and a marshmallowy inside, while icing sugar produces a marshmallowy result inside and out. Passionfruit curd is a rich, buttery spread that is very versatile and has an intense, fruity flavour. This curd recipe is quite tart to offset the sweetness of the pavlova, but if you wish, you can add some more sugar.

Preheat the oven to 120°C (Gas ¼–½).

Place the egg whites, cream of tartar and vanilla in a large, clean, dry bowl. Using an electric mixer, beat on high for 2–3 minutes, or until stiff.

Add the sugar ¼ cup at a time, beating well after each addition, until the mixture is thick and glossy. You'll know your mix is perfect by tasting a little – it should be smooth and not gritty. Next, add the cornflour and vinegar and beat until combined.

Take two baking trays and dot ½ teaspoon of the meringue mix onto each corner. Line the trays with baking paper, sticking the paper down in each corner.

Using a large spoon, scoop out some of the meringue mix and place on the baking tray. Pile the mixture up as high as possible and don't flatten it. Repeat this process until you have formed 8 mini pavlovas about 6 cm in diameter. Be sure to leave a 10 cm gap between the pavlovas, as they may spread out during the cooking process.

Bake on the middle and bottom shelves of the oven for 40 minutes, or until lightly golden. Turn off the heat and allow the pavlovas to cool in the oven for 30 minutes with the door closed, then remove the pavlovas using oven mitts and allow to cool completely.

To make the passionfruit curd, strain the pulp over a small saucepan to remove the seeds (you should be left with about ¼ cup of juice). Add the lemon juice and butter and melt over medium heat, stirring well with a wooden spoon.

Whisk together the sugar and egg yolks in a medium bowl for a few minutes, or until frothy. Add to the passionfruit and butter mix, turn the heat to low and whisk continuously for about 5 minutes, or until the mixture is thick. Transfer to a small bowl and refrigerate until cold.

To serve, top each pavlova with whipped cream, a drizzle of passionfruit curd, some slices of banana and some passionfruit pulp.

Apple enchiladas

Mexico

Medium

5

Serves

I made these with my cooking school students and they absolutely loved them. Invite all your friends over one weekend and make these together – they'll be a hit! You could also use raspberries, strawberries, fresh peaches or preserved cherries instead of the apple as a filling – just omit the spices and walnuts in this case.

Preheat the oven to 180ºC (Gas 4). Grease a baking tray with the butter, using some scrunched-up baking paper.

To make the caramel sauce, place the butter, sugar and water in a medium saucepan over medium heat and bring to the boil. Continue to boil, stirring constantly with a wooden spoon, for 5 minutes. Remove from the heat and leave to cool.

Place the apples on a chopping board, with the cored holes facing upwards. Using a sharp knife, slice them in half vertically, and place the pieces cut sides down on the chopping board. Slice each apple into thin slivers and put in a bowl.

Melt the butter in a frying pan over low heat. Add the sugar, cinnamon, nutmeg and vanilla. Stir until all the sugar has dissolved.

Next, add the apple and walnuts and stir well. Cover with a lid and cook, stirring occasionally, for about 15 minutes, or until the apples are quite soft but still retaining their shape.

Lay the tortillas on a baking tray and place in the oven for 1 minute to soften (this will make the tortillas easier to roll up).

Evenly spoon the cooked apple in a straight line down the middle of each tortilla. Tightly roll them into sausage shapes and place seam side down on the greased baking tray. Evenly ladle the cooled caramel sauce over the enchiladas, making sure every part is completely covered. Sprinkle with a little of the extra cinnamon.

Bake on the middle shelf of the oven for about 20 minutes. Watch the enchiladas carefully so that they don't burn – they should come out crisp on top but not too toasty!

Remove from the oven using oven mitts. Using an egg flip, arrange the enchiladas on serving plates. Serve straight away with some double cream or vanilla ice-cream, if desired.

1 teaspoon **butter**, for greasing

8 **granny smith apples**, peeled and cored

30 g **butter**

2 tablespoons **brown sugar**

½ teaspoon **ground cinnamon**

½ teaspoon **ground nutmeg**

1 tablespoon **vanilla extract**

2 tablespoons **walnuts**, crushed

10 small flour **tortillas***

extra **ground cinnamon**, to garnish

double cream or **vanilla ice-cream** (optional), to serve

CARAMEL SAUCE
70 g **butter**
½ cup **brown sugar**
100 ml **water**

EQUIPMENT
baking paper
baking tray
measuring spoons
measuring cups
measuring jug
medium saucepan
wooden spoon
chopping board
sharp knife
medium mixing bowl
frying pan with lid
ladle
oven mitts
egg flip

Some of the native foods found in Mexico include vanilla beans, avocados, cacao beans and chillis.

Bread and butter pudding

1 teaspoon **butter**, for greasing

10 slices of **raisin bread**

1 **large apple**, peeled, cored and very thinly sliced

1 teaspoon **ground cinnamon**

2 cups **milk**

¾ cup **brown sugar**

20 g **butter**

3 **eggs**

1 tablespoon **vanilla extract**

double cream or **vanilla ice-cream**, to serve

EQUIPMENT

measuring spoons

sharp knife

chopping board

baking paper

23 cm square baking dish

measuring cups

medium saucepan

wooden spoon

whisk

medium mixing bowl

ladle

foil

skewer

oven mitts

Bread and butter pudding is definitely the right dish to make when you feel like eating dessert but can't be bothered spending a long time in the kitchen! I recommend using a granny smith or red delicious apple in this recipe. And at Easter, you could use hot cross buns instead of the raisin bread for a seasonal dessert.

Preheat the oven to 170ºC (Gas 3). Grease a 23 cm square baking dish with the butter, using some scrunched-up baking paper.

Cut each slice of bread into four squares. Arrange half of the bread on the base of the dish so that the pieces are overlapping. Layer the apple on top of the bread, then sprinkle over half the cinnamon.

Combine the milk, sugar and butter in a saucepan over medium heat and stir with a wooden spoon until the butter has melted and the sugar has dissolved.

Whisk the eggs and the vanilla in a medium bowl. Ask an adult to slowly drizzle in the hot milk while you quickly whisk (this will ensure that the eggs don't cook from the heat).

Ladle half of the egg mixture over the bread. Arrange the remaining bread on top, again overlapping the pieces. Top with the remaining cinnamon and egg mixture.

Cover the dish with foil and bake for 45 minutes, or until a skewer inserted into the centre of the pudding comes out fairly clean.

Remove the dish from the oven using oven mitts and leave to settle for 10 minutes. Serve with a dollop of double cream or a scoop of vanilla ice-cream.

simply delicious!

How to julienne

The term julienne refers to a French cooking method that produces matchstick-thin slices of vegetables. To julienne, first cut off the roots, stems, seeds or other inedible parts of the vegetable and peel if required. Next, cut your vegetable in half and position the cut side down on a chopping board, so it doesn't slip. Cut off any rounded edges from each side and discard. Cut ½ cm thin strips lengthways. Stack these strips on top of each other and repeat, cutting these strips into ½ cm thick lengthways slices.

What is blind baking?

Dried beans or uncooked rice are often used to weigh down a pastry case when it is being cooked in the oven. The weight you place on the pastry prevents it from bubbling up and keeps it in the desired shape.

It is important to properly line the pastry with baking paper first before putting in the beans or rice. If not, your beans or rice will cook into the pastry and you'll have the time-consuming job of picking them all out before using the pastry shell!

You can also buy commercial pie weights. They're essentially little ceramic balls that weigh down your pastry. I prefer using these as I find them easier and less messy to work with. Rice or beans that have been used as pie weights can be re-used time and time again. Just store them in a jar and re-use as needed.

What is simmering and what is a rolling boil?

Simmering refers to the state where water gently bubbles away when heat is applied. This state first occurs just as the water starts to boil. If the heat is turned down straight away, it will continue to simmer.

A **rolling boil** refers to water that is boiling aggressively. There are two ways you can tell whether or not you have a rolling boil. First, look for large bubbles that keep on forming and coming to the surface. Second, stir the water with a wooden spoon – if you have a rolling boil, the water will keep on boiling the same way when you stir it and there will be no variation in bubbles appearing. A rolling boil is needed to cook pasta or vegetables.

How to slice something that has just come out of the oven

First, if you've just started cooking and using an oven, it's a good idea to ask an adult to take things out of the oven for you. If you're taking the dish out yourself, don't forget to use oven mitts! Once out, allow the dish to cool for 5–10 minutes on your stovetop. Next, ask an adult or friend to wear oven mitts and hold the dish very steadily for you as you slice. Keeping your elbows up (so you don't accidentally lean on the dish), slice the dish into portions. Watch out for any steam that may escape as you cut. Use a long-handled egg flip to scoop out portions and serve.

How to blitz onion or garlic to a paste

Blitzing means using a food processor to chop up an ingredient very finely so that it turns into a paste. First, place the peeled onion and/or garlic into the bowl of a food processor. Put the lid on tightly and process for at least 1 minute. You'll need to stop the food processor a couple of times during the blitzing, take off the lid and scrape down the sides with a spatula. This mixes in any big bits that have crept away from the blades! When ready, carefully take the blade out of the bowl and use a spatula to scrape out the paste.

Why use the middle shelf of the oven?

Food cooks the most quickly and evenly when placed on the middle shelf of an oven. This is because hot air rises through the middle shelf and goes through the cake (or whatever else you're cooking) on its way to the top. Also, the middle of the oven has the most consistent and accurate temperature. Before you heat your oven, make sure that you position a shelf in the middle ready for cooking!

How to tell when something is 'al dente'

'Al dente' is an Italian term meaning 'tender to the bite'. 'Al dente' pasta or rice is soft enough to comfortably bite into (and eat!) but is still firm enough to hold its shape. Keep on tasting the pasta or rice as it nears the end of its cooking time. When it's just tender all the way through, and isn't gluggy on the outside, it should be ready.

How to measure dry ingredients (in cups or spoons)

Select a commercial measuring cup or spoon. Spoon out or take a large scoop of your dry ingredient so that it overfills. (Do not pack in the ingredient unless you're measuring brown sugar.) Use a palette knife (or the flat edge of a butter knife) to smooth out and level the top. This ensures that you are measuring ingredients accurately, which is especially important when baking!

How to work flour into a dough

Work quickly but gently when making scone, damper or gnocchi dough. It's important not to bang down, squeeze or squash hard. Ideally you should mix the flour in, a little at a time, until just lightly combined. If you overwork it you will activate too much gluten in the dough, which means your food may turn out chewy and tough! It's also important to note that sometimes you may not need all the flour specified in the recipe to get the right result (especially when making gnocchi). With practice you'll get the hang of knowing when a dough mixture feels right or needs more flour.

How to cream butter and sugar

Place softened butter and caster sugar into a large ceramic bowl. Using an electric hand-held mixer, mix the butter and sugar on low for the first minute, then on high for the next 4 minutes. As you mix, you will see the butter lighten in colour. The mixture will also get creamier and fluffier as it incorporates the sugar. You will need to stop halfway through the creaming process to scrape down the sides of your bowl with a spatula. This ensures that all the mixture is properly incorporated.

Glossary of ingredients

Couscous

Couscous is a staple food of North Africa. It's also very popular in the Middle East. Made from semolina (the hard part of ground wheat), flour, salt and water, couscous is similar to very small pasta.

Cream of tartar

This is an acidic salt compound used in cooking. It stabilises egg whites during the beating process (meaning it helps keep them stiff) and also helps increase their volume. It also makes frostings creamier by helping to prevent any hard, sugary crystals forming. It has no odour and is white in colour.

Fried shallots

Fried shallots are a garnish popular in many Asian dishes. They're thinly sliced and deep-fried until they turn golden and crispy. Readily available from supermarkets and Asian food stores, they should be stored in an airtight container and used within 3–4 weeks after opening.

Garam masala

This Indian spice mixture can be purchased pre-made, but it's also easy to make at home (see page 58). While garam masala varies from region to region, it typically includes cinnamon, nutmeg, cloves and other spices. If you have time, it's always better to use a mortar and pestle and grind the whole spices yourself rather than using pre-ground spices.

Girello

Girello is the Italian word for the eye of a round of beef that lends itself well to slow cooking. It forms one part of silverside and is very lean.

Jasmine rice

This is a fragrant long-grain rice that has a subtle, nutty taste. Jasmine rice is widely used in Thai and Chinese cuisines. It's best used within 6 months of purchase, as it tends to lose its aroma after this time and become slightly woody.

Madras curry powder

This is a spicy curry powder that originates from the south of India. It was named after the Indian city of Madras, which has subsequently been renamed Chennai. If you're not used to spicy foods it might be a good idea to go easy on the Madras curry powder to begin with.

Mirin

Mirin is a sweet rice wine that is used a lot in Japanese cooking. It's similar to the Japanese wine sake but has a lower alcohol content. Mirin can be bought from the Asian section of most supermarkets.

Orange blossom water

This is a traditional ingredient used in Middle Eastern cooking. Also known as orange flower water, this clear liquid is a distillation of fresh blossoms from orange trees. Its use is now becoming much more widespread, with countries such as France and Greece using it to flavour desserts.

Potato flour

This flour is made using potato that has been cooked, mashed and dried. The dried potato is then ground, producing a light flour that contains both the starch and protein component of potatoes. It is off-white in colour and should not be confused with potato starch, which is similar to cornflour and has a different purpose in cooking.

Preserved lemon

This is lemon that has been preserved in brine made from water, lemon juice and lots of salt. The preserving process can take several months and produces a very intense lemony result. Preserved lemons are popular in Moroccan cuisine where they are traditionally used in tagines (dishes cooked in clay pots). They should be rinsed well before use and used sparingly as their flavour is very intense!

Raspberry vinegar

Raspberry vinegar is made by steeping whole, fresh raspberries in white wine vinegar. The vinegar is left for a little over a week, then the liquid is drained off into a saucepan. An equal part of sugar is added and the liquid is boiled down for 5–8 minutes. It has many uses in cooking, suiting both sweet and savoury dishes.

Red capsicum paste

Made from red capsicums (peppers), salt, olive oil and garlic, this intense concentrated paste is perfect for adding to stews, meats and many other fish and vegetable dishes. Also known as red pepper paste, it takes 24–48 hours to make. It is used in numerous cuisines, most notably Middle Eastern and Portuguese, and is available from specialty food stores.

Souvlaki bread

Souvlaki bread is a type of flatbread that is typically softer than pita bread. Made from wheat, it has a slight yellowy tinge to it. The bread is usually heated slightly before it's filled to make wrapping up ingredients even easier.

Tamarind paste

Tamarind paste is a thick, sticky fruit pulp that has a well-balanced sweet and sour flavour. It comes from a tamarind tree that is native to Africa. Its fruit (where the paste is extracted from) resembles brown pea pods. The riper the fruit, the sweeter the pulp it yields. It's one of the many ingredients that make up Worcestershire sauce.

Tortillas

This is a type of round flatbread made from wheat or corn. It's very popular in Mexico where it is filled with meat and vegetables. The word 'tortilla' is also used to describe a type of omelette in Spain and South America.

Tzatziki

This refreshing dip is made from plain yoghurt, grated cucumber, garlic, olive oil, salt and pepper. Sometimes other flavourings such as lemon juice are added. It is traditionally eaten in Greece and Turkey.

Udon noodles

Udon noodles are very common ingredient in Japan. They are white in colour and are made from wheat flour, salt and water. You can buy both dried or fresh udon noodles. In my cooking, I use dried udon noodles as they're generally thinner than the fresh ones and are also less doughy.

Vialone nano rice

A short-grain risotto rice that is high in starch, which is what makes risotto incredibly creamy. Vialone nano is considered by many to be the best risotto rice, superior to others such as arborio. It holds together well and yields some bite when cooked. It's available from Italian and specialty food stores.

Start your applause ...

Many authors say that the hardest part of writing a book is the 'starting bit'. Just thinking about the work that's ahead of you is enough to strike fear into any person's heart.

In saying this, one way to get started is if you know someone has your back at all times! My husband, Anthony, has helped me in more ways than I can count. The amount of support he has offered me has been unparalleled and that is why he is mentioned first here and this book is dedicated to him. You da man!

Huge thanks go to my mum, for being passionate about good food and sharing all her knowledge with me. She really is a fabulous cook. No doubt about it.

To my younger brother and sister J-Man (James) and Missy (Mia) who (at the time of printing!) were 12 and 11 years old respectively. Thanks for being my taste testers when I was developing these recipes and for giving me your valuable feedback. Love you guys!

To the rest of my family and friends who have inspired and supported my culinary journey over the years – thank you all!

Without any shadow of a doubt, it's because of the legendary Nigella Lawson that I felt inspired enough to write about food on a daily basis. Over a decade ago, her book *How to Eat* completely changed the way I thought, talked about and enjoyed food.

To my publisher Paul, thank you for looking after my book. To be given one opportunity to write a book was amazing, but to be asked to come back and produce another work is one of my proudest moments. To my editor Jane – I've really, really enjoyed working with you! To my photographer John, food-stylist Deb and designer Trisha – what a dream to have all of your mind-boggling talent pumped into this book.

And finally to all of the customers who have supported Little Kitchen by buying my books and products across the world – thank you for enabling me to do what I love to do, which is to be involved with food on such a personal level.

Sabrina Parrini

As a child, Sabrina learnt how to make perfect potato gnocchi from her mother, succulent roast chicken from her paternal grandmother and polenta with ragu from her maternal grandmother. Luckily for Sabrina, her Italian family kept her well fed and well educated in all things culinary.

Growing up, it was always with a hearty chuckle that her grandmother fondly remembered Sabrina's early love of food. She loved to recount the time when the toddler Sabrina ran innumerable, excited laps around the family's dedicated 'dessert table' one Christmas, impatient that the food was taking so long to be served! To this day, a good spread never fails to disappoint and, as an adult, her early enthusiasm for food remains unchanged.

After completing a teaching degree, Sabrina established her own organic children's cookery school and designed Australia's first range of 'child-inspired' cookware. Her love of teaching children to cook has been translated into her own children's cookbooks, with her first book, *Little Kitchen*, published in 2009.

Sabrina is a guest presenter on children's television program *Kitchen Whiz*. She lives, writes and cooks in the Australian countryside, in a beautiful home with a big kitchen and a culinary garden.

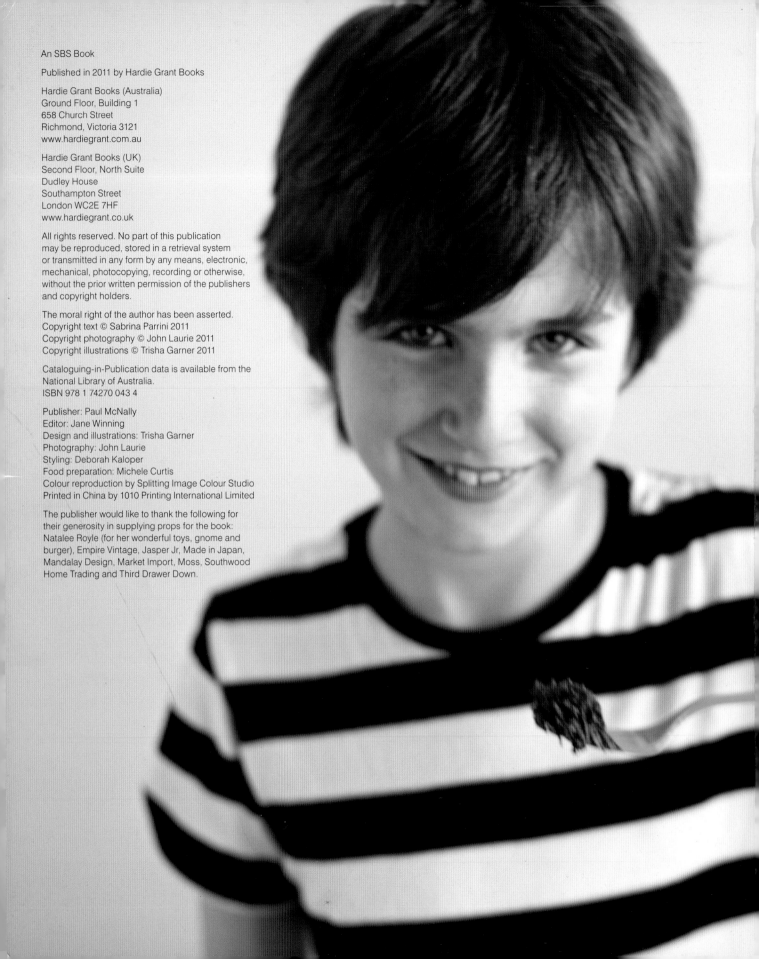

An SBS Book

Published in 2011 by Hardie Grant Books

Hardie Grant Books (Australia)
Ground Floor, Building 1
658 Church Street
Richmond, Victoria 3121
www.hardiegrant.com.au

Hardie Grant Books (UK)
Second Floor, North Suite
Dudley House
Southampton Street
London WC2E 7HF
www.hardiegrant.co.uk

Cataloguing-in-Publication data is available from the
National Library of Australia.
ISBN 978 1 74270 043 4

Publisher: Paul McNally
Editor: Jane Winning
Design and illustrations: Trisha Garner
Photography: John Laurie
Styling: Deborah Kaloper
Food preparation: Michele Curtis
Colour reproduction by Splitting Image Colour Studio
Printed in China by 1010 Printing International Limited

The publisher would like to thank the following for
their generosity in supplying props for the book:
Natalee Royle (for her wonderful toys, gnome and
burger), Empire Vintage, Jasper Jr, Made in Japan,
Mandalay Design, Market Import, Moss, Southwood
Home Trading and Third Drawer Down.